21st Century Japan Decoded:

The only Manual on Mental Health for Blacks in Japan

By

Takuan Amaru

21ˢᵗ Century Japan Decoded:

The only Manual on Mental Health for Blacks in Japan

by Takuan Amaru

Published by AfroAsiatic Books

Nagoya, Japan

www.afroasiatic.jp
www.takuanamaru.com

Amaru, Takuan

21ˢᵗ Century Japan Decoded: The only Manual on Mental Health for Blacks in Japan

Includes bibliographical references and index

ISBN: 978-4-908556-10-4

21st Century Japan Decoded:

The only Manual on Mental Health for Blacks in Japan

Table of Contents

Prologue

As a boy, living in the United States, I was oftentimes teased about my Japanese heritage. Among the 'chink jokes' I had to endure, the one I hated most was being called *Jap*. The last time I got into a fight over this, the teacher that broke up the altercation (who happened to be a black woman), dropped a gem of knowledge which forever changed my perspective on the idea of accepting derogatory epithets. "I'm sick of him calling me "Jap!" I insisted as she led me to the vice principal's office. "Oh, is that all?" she replied before gently placing a hand on my shoulder to stop me. After turning in my direction, she then bent slightly at the waist and rested both hands on her knees. Even though it was clear the woman wanted me to look at her, I made her wait a couple seconds before raising my head. Having made eye-contact, once the woman was confident she held my attention, only then did she speak. "Young man, don't ever forget this," she said in a tone of urgency. "It's not what anyone calls you, it's what you answer to." Then she paused to look further. "Well? Are you a Jap?" Stunned by her question I was stumped for a reply. The woman, sensing my frustration, resumed. "If not, why are you responding? He's not talking to you, is he? He's talking to a 'Jap'—whatever that is."

In Japan, the script has been flipped.

Nowadays, Japanese want to label me *hafu* or *gaijin*. Many foreigners in Japan don't mind being called gaijin. To each his/her own but when I observe these people, based on their words, actions, and mannerisms, I cannot help but notice how the majority of them seem to suffer from issues of insecurity and low self-esteem. This debate about whether or not 'gaijin' is acceptable brings to mind how back in the day, in my neighborhood, some of my friends greeted me by saying, *"What's up fool?"* Now, in the right context, I never considered this to be rude or demeaning. However this is a far cry from saying it was okay for everyone to call me a fool. Taken a step further, if anyone were to identify with 'fool' (or Jap) to the point they responded whenever they heard it, don't you think this would be psychologically damaging? In my opinion, accepting the label of gaijin, along with everything embedded within this designation, is nearly the same.

Blueprint: Words of Wisdom

The following paragraph is my personal rendition of a verse originally composed by Queen Mother Spirit Change a.k.a. Dr. Dora Gray, alongside her king, Baba Wesley Jehuti Gray. During the past decade, like many of you, I've had the opportunity to meet some interesting people via social media. Baba Jehuti is one such person. Considering how *Facebook*, *Instagram*, *Twitter*, and other networks span the globe, it is no wonder that I've encountered the entire spectrum when it comes to personalities: everything from outgoing, extroverted, and extremely hedonistic to shy, conservative, religious, and even some pious scholars and elder statesmen. If I have to choose which of these categories Baba Jehuti falls into, it is certainly the latter. African drummer, griot, music historian, husband, and father, although I've never had the pleasure of actually meeting the man in-person, I am persuaded to see him as a sort of father figure. In melanin-rich society, at the adult-stage of development, every capable man assumes the role of 'father' in the community. This has nothing to do with whether or not a man biologically gives birth to his own children. If you are on Baba Jehuti's list of friends, you are privy to a wealth of soulfully uplifting anecdotes, articles on musical history, and other information concerning Black people. In my opinion, the voice in which he communicates his message is akin to how loving fathers address family members. Considering the poetically eloquent statement below was created by his queen and endorsed by him, this only adds to the balanced feeling of love and parental guidance. Now, when this queen and king inked these thoughts onto paper, I have no reason to believe that either of them had blacks who live in Japan on their mind. Nevertheless, considering how any 'real truth' cannot be limited to a single instance but instead is a universal principle, while I was reading their words of wisdom, the spirit of my ancestors plucked me on the noggin to say that contained therein is the blueprint for *21st Century Japan Decoded.*

Do you know that when you accept the words/actions/beliefs of close-minded people, you are compromising a part of yourself which is needed to fulfill your higher purpose? Upon arriving to Japan, you almost certainly will have to temporarily tolerate the 'gaijin-treatment,' especially at school or work, until you become familiar with your new environment. Feeling alienated is oftentimes chalked-up as culture shock. Nevertheless, in far too many instances, separation from the group subjects a person to immature, disrespectful, or otherwise distasteful behavior. During these challenging moments remember who you are and do not stoop to their level by responding in kind. Forgive them, but make it clear this situation is not acceptable. You have not journeyed to this island-nation to be abused by those who routinely demean others so they can feel better about their own insecurities. Physically or mentally distance yourself from people who are consistently out-of-pocket until they are permanently removed from your thoughts. Please remember, whenever someone—Japanese or not—attempts to disrespect you, they are operating at a very low vibrational frequency and, in the process, unknown to them, they are raising yours. Were they operating at a higher frequency, and truly understood the Law of Karma, they would not dare to be so insolent. Always thank the Most High for the lessons which appear in the form of challenges and never forget who you are. Lastly, remember to shun taking things personally from those who do not know you, for they only speak from their very limited opinions. Avoid overreacting by committing an offense you may later regret because, at the end of the day,

Prologue

the bed you make is the very same one you will have to sleep in... You are blessed! Be at peace. With much love.

~Takuan Amaru

Introduction

The overwhelming pressure felt by superstar athlete, Naomi Osaka, which led to her controversial withdrawals of grand slam tournaments over "mental depression" and "suffering long bouts of depression," is symbolic of the experience of both Blacks (worldwide) and Japanese people. By reading the responses to Osaka's tweets by members of the dominant society, it is evident that many feel she has no choice other than to endure whatever they dish out. This, regardless of the negative effects on her psyche. In other words, a large part of her being accepted is to feebly surrender to their whims. This has absolutely nothing to do with the sport of tennis but, rather, maintaining the status-quo.

Unlike in the West, where societally derived pressure can be direct and in-your-face, in Japan, mounting stress is oftentimes so passive and indirect its victims are wholly unaware they are under attack until it is too late. This is analogous to the premise of the frog in a pot of water which is gradually heated. The heat is turned up so slowly the frog is oblivious of any danger and, therefore, fails to save itself by simply jumping out. In the past two decades, I have met several foreign nationals on this island-nation who fall into this category. Some of them, over time, have become so far removed from reality they can no longer relate to the people in their home countries. Having been fully indoctrinated into their roles as non-threatening *gaijin*, instead of maturing into shining examples of the greatness of their people, they have either been reduced to feeble, harmless minorities who resemble *kawaii* mascots like *Kumamon*, or they have descended to the other extreme and have become overly withdrawn and bitter.

Over the years, I have received hundreds of texts and emails inquiring what it is like for a black person to live in Japan. Some of the questions are about the food, culture, or language. However the number one concern people have is whether or not Japanese—the people themselves—are racist against dark-skinned people. To me, this has always blown my mind considering the folks asking these questions are usually from card-carrying white supremacist nations like the U.K. or the U.S.A. Following the racism topic, the next subjects of concern involve socializing with Japanese as well as how they communicate to one another. And, not surprisingly, many are curious about romantic endeavors such as dating. *21st Century Japan Decoded* touches on these subjects. But please understand the focus of the book is to provide guidance for blacks who are residing here from the perspective of mental-health.

Japan's increasing negative-birthrate is shrinking the native-population at such an alarming pace that augmenting the workforce with foreigners has become a priority of the government. While much of the immigrant influx is from Asian nations such as China, South Korea, or the Philippines, due to Japan's commitment to global expansion and technological development, opportunities for university graduates from western nations, including the non-stop need for native-English teachers, have become permanent fixtures. As opposed to past years when few career options existed in Japan, nowadays, more and more foreign nationals are deciding to settle down here. Considering Japan's astronomical suicide rate is no secret, it should not be controversial to say something peculiar is taking place behind closed doors. Editorials on the darker-side of society, especially those detailing the psychotic maladies consistently trending in the news like *Ijime* (bullying), *Hikikomori* (hermitage), *Karoshi* (death from overworking), or *Kodokushi* (dying all alone) normally conclude with blanket-statements that place the blame on undue stress. After hearing explanations by government officials, psychiatrists, or other experts, the only thing listeners really come away with is there is an overwhelming amount of pressure in the society, but almost nothing concerning possible approaches that may save a person's life such as discussing intervention methods or other such preventative measures.

What does this mean for black people in Japan?

Furthermore, from a mental-health perspective, in such a high-pressure environment wherein bias against foreigners is as traditional as *haiku* or *soba* (noodles), is it possible for them to maintain a sense of self-worth and dignity? If the culture really fosters some sort of unique pressure, and if what I suggest about accepting the gaijin label is true, with increasing numbers of blacks settling here, this could result in a rising level of mental illness. Anyone familiar with psychological disorders understands most types of neurosis do not become full-blown cases overnight. Although severe mental trauma can be the result of just one incident of rape or mugging, usually people who exhibit sociopathic behavior gradually acquire their condition over a number of weeks, months, years, or even decades. Taking this into account, the goal of this book is to explain the framework of the society, including the behavioral pattern of its inhabitants, so any properly informed person can diagnose their surroundings and make the necessary adjustments to their living situation that will result in a sound, healthy state-of-mind. In easy-to-understand words, the reader is provided insight to common challenges as well as access to tried-and-true methods that allow a person to align their attitude and actions 'with the flow' of society—this as opposed to vainly attempting to 'swim upstream' against an invincible tide of negativity and disapproval. For the practitioner, attaining this level of stability within such a stressful environment creates a safe space to have what the great scholar, Chancellor Williams, calls the "time to think."

"In short, certain conditions can bring about that internal peace, stability, and confidence which unshackle the mind. There is now time to think."

~ Chancellor Williams

To do this requires a fundamental understanding of not only Japanese society but also of ourselves. Therefore this book takes both sides into account. First, in part 1, we will explore the dark, all-pervasive cloud encompassing Japan: the cause of mental illness and their unique complex. For Japanese, stress is a daily factor that is *supposed* to affect every person's actions and behavior. For this reason, it is not farfetched to say Japanese consider feelings of extreme pressure to be as natural a phenomenon as breathing oxygen. This ties into the mental condition known as the *Japanese Complex*: their innate psychological response to the atomic bombings of Hiroshima and Nagasaki. It incorporates all of the post-war trauma, especially the humiliating treatment by the United States. From a historical perspective, it could be

Introduction

said Japan never really abolished the *Sakoku Edicts* that, for over 200 years, banned Europeans from the island. Although gaijin are no longer outright slain or expelled, I oftentimes hear Westerners complain how they never feel accepted by the society. This is due to the *Yamato Code*: the code of ethics that dictate the behavior of Japanese. Part 3 is a detailed breakdown of the Code. However, prior to this, in part 2, the tables get turned as we discuss black issues and the types of foreigners who typically make their home in Japan. Part 4, which is the final section, summarizes our findings and addresses much of the adversity commonly encountered in Japan—including racial profiling by police—with real-time, practical solutions. Please remember this book is a self-help, self-improvement guide. The objective is to identify potential issues, hazards, or situations that can lead to mental illness and, more importantly, to prescribe preventative measures and remedies. To accomplish this, it is necessary for the reader to take a good-hard-look at themselves; so if you are not open to reflecting on and confronting your own issues and shortcomings, this book may not be for you. This is because the problem-solving methods will only be effective for those who are committed to achieving a certain sense of self-awareness and dignity.

Part 1: Mental Health in Japan

Chapter 1: Duplicity

"*Japanese people are two-faced.*" As a child, my mother would never fail to remind me of this whenever we were visiting a Japanese person's home. "If you are offered something to eat, you must politely decline," she would insist, "even if you're hungry." If I accepted anything on the first or second offer, I would be scolded after we got home. According to her, if the person asked three times, this would confirm the sincerity of their offer to prepare some food for me. Otherwise, she claimed, it is just *tatemae*. The duality of *Tatemae* (建前) vs. *Honne* (本音), which is the politically correct behavior Japanese exhibit in public versus the real thoughts in their heart, to put it mildly, was confusing to a boy growing up outside of Japan. The extreme population density of the island-nation (nearly 350 inhabitants per km²) has forced its residents, throughout the centuries, to practically live on top of one another. And when you consider until the Meiji Era the houses were made of thin wood with paper (*shoji*) doors, in addition to the close proximity of these homes to the sidewalk or street, you may begin to understand the mindset of a people who devised a system which prioritizes formal responses and behavior rather than risking offending others by saying what is on their mind. Does this 'sugarcoating of the truth' result in achieving harmony? Perhaps. But we must admit that communicating in such a round-about way also has the propensity to lead to misunderstanding. What cannot be denied is, in many cases, this need to be indirect causes stressful situations.

The Myth of Japan being a Safe Country

This may be viewed as controversial but here it goes: every Japanese person is at least slightly psychotic—and there are no exceptions. Being required to repress their own self-expression and identity (*tatemae*), just this on-going daily pressure to conform results in a form of neurosis. Once you become familiar with the symptoms, hints of their social condition can be seen almost anywhere. You can clearly see it whenever Japanese repeat-back to foreigners something they believe 'everyone knows.' An example of this is when they express pride about how safe Japan is, all the while knowing this is not true. Okay, perhaps when it comes to physical threats from strangers (i.e. getting mugged, etc.). But what about in terms of mental health? Just a cursory glance at the rate of suicide—in some years over 90 people a day— suggests that in regards to mental health Japan is anything but safe. There are even certified "suicide spots" all throughout the country such as Aokigahara Forest, which is on the northwestern slope of Mount Fuji in Yamanashi Prefecture, and Shin-Koiwa Station in Tokyo. Some of these locations are so infamous that tours are available for visitors. In 1998, the annual cases of Japanese taking their own lives topped 30,000 deaths; and in 2003 this figure peaked at 34,427. Since then, to relieve some of the stress, many of the larger companies have taken preventive measures such as limiting the amount of overtime and making it mandatory for employees to take paid-holidays. Nevertheless considering that a 'good year' concerning suicide deaths is anything below 25,000, it can be reasonably asserted that whatever is causing pressure in Japanese society is still alive and well.

As for non-Japanese, a research paper on suicide rates among foreign residents in Japan was published in 2019 by Stuart Gilmour, Haruko Hoshino, and Bibha Dhungel. Their findings indicated that, other than Korean nationals, suicide rates for the international community were considerably lower than Japanese residents. "We found that suicide mortality among Korean nationals living in Japan is significantly higher than that of Japanese nationals, even after adjusting for age… By contrast, Chinese nationals living in Japan have lower suicide mortality rates than Japanese after adjusting for age, and their suicide mortality rate is not significantly different than that of their home country." Since *21st Century Japan Decoded* focuses on the well-being of melanin-rich nationals, it is the final sentences of the report which caught my attention: "Nationals of other countries in Japan have lower suicide mortality rates than Japanese nationals, and their suicide mortality rate is also lower than the global rate after standardization. These patterns held for men and women." According to this report, most people might agree that suicide rates in 2019 were not a major concern for blacks. But what about by the year 2030? Or 2040? With black people now residing in Japan in greater numbers, isn't it likely that sooner or later they, too, will succumb to the same mental-health issues which plague Japanese?

Medical News Today journalist, Adam Felman, defines the word 'health' as a state of complete emotional and physical well-being. He calls it the "optimal state of health." To even have a chance of achieving this requires a harmonious, nurturing environment to live in—one which is safe from *both* a physical and emotional standpoint. Back in the 1990s, when I served as a mental-health specialist at the Children's Transitional Residence (C.T.R.), which is a facility of the University of Behavioral Healthcare in Piscataway, New Jersey, I would scoff at some of the clinical approaches that were used to instruct the children. Methodology such as giving them 'time-outs' for being naughty, or awarding them 'points' for good behavior. In spite of this, having grown up in a home that was less-than-stable from an emotional well-being perspective, the idea of creating a 'safe environment' really attracted me.

So what is a safe environment?

According to The United States Institute of Peace (U.S.I.P.), an American federal institution tasked with promoting conflict resolution and prevention worldwide, a safe and secure environment is: "one in which the population has the freedom to pursue daily activities without fear of politically motivated, persistent, or large-scale violence. Such an environment is characterized by an end to large-scale fighting; an adequate level of public order; the subordination of accountable security forces to legitimate state authority; the protection of key individuals, communities, sites, and infrastructure; and the freedom for people and goods to move about the country and across borders without fear of undue harm to life and limb."

This definition addresses safety in a physical sense, which means as long as the threat of danger is coming from somewhere *outside* of oneself, i.e. muggers, rapists, etc. Relatively speaking, to prevent crimes of this nature is not so complicated. Installing alarms and video cameras, hiring security, getting a dog or a gun, any of these may serve as solutions to keep thugs and murderers where they should be: outside of your safety zone. But what about when the source of danger (i.e. the bad guy) is no longer outside the borders of protection but, instead, has penetrated the castle walls and now resides *inside* of your very own psyche? Whenever a person's mental/emotional safety comes under threat there is no longer any chance of keeping the criminal out. This is simply because, in this case, the victim and the bad guy have now become one and the same person.

During the last decade, think-tanks in Norway who are concerned with the emotional stability of its citizens have defined Societal Safety as: "The society's ability to maintain critical social functions, to protect the life and health of the citizens and to meet the citizens' basic requirements in a variety of stress situations." Furthermore, it is stated that the aim of societal safety is to implement "a systematic approach for understanding, mitigating, and responding to social problems such as extraordinary stresses and losses, interferences in complex and mutual dependent systems, or lack of trust in vital social institutions." Japanese society is known for being *dantaiteki* (団体的), which means having a strong sense of group cohesion. Later we shall explore this fundamental trait of the culture but, for the time being, please note that one of the ramifications of this dynamic is alienating foreigners or anyone not deemed a member of the group. Please note Japanese are not exempt from what I call *otherization*; and this is evident in the high number of suicides by people who are marginalized by their fellow countrymen through some form of *ijime* (bullying). A writer on global health and behavioral science, Nicole F. Roberts, writes: "Heartbreak, loss, or being left out are particularly difficult to process for humans as social creatures. But the impact is not only limited to how the brain processes the emotions and pain associated with rejection. There is also evidence that suggests not being able to 'think straight' is a real outcome of feeling rejected." In addition to exhibiting less self-control and becoming more aggressive, the article also mentions research from Case Western Reserve University indicating a significant drop in IQ levels by 25% and an "immediate drop" in reasoning by 30%."

According to this data, does Japan still seem so safe?

Since the objective of this book is to put the reader inside the mind of typical Japanese for the purpose of exploring their way of thinking, let's start by asking a simple question. How did Japanese get to the point where they have been instinctively wired with the mentality to keep foreigners out? Upon arriving to Japan, every non-Japanese is immediately exposed to a passive form of being alienated: the *otherized* treatment. And this indoctrination begins right away, in the first interactions with coworkers or whomever they happen to meet. Most are unaware that Japanese—even the friendliest and most open-minded—do this unconsciously due to their post-traumatic stress from the war which has resulted in a psychological complex.

Chapter 2: The Japanese Complex

Throughout history, Japanese have been known for having a xenophobic mindset toward foreigners. That said, there is a peculiar complex which, I believe, is only activated by Westerners—especially English-speaking natives. It is debatable as to whether this complex came into existence back in 1853 as the result of Commodore Matthew Perry forcing the Japanese government to open its borders, ending its 220-year-policy excluding Europeans, or following World War II. In 1952, a year after General Douglas MacArthur and his Supreme Command of the Allied Powers (S.C.A.P.) ended their seven-year occupation and departed the island-nation, Japan fully regained its independence—at least on paper. However, in spite of having their sovereignty reinstated, they remained a broken nation in search of a new identity. After being granted membership in the United Nations in 1956, Japan showcased its economic and infrastructure rebuilding when the world paid Tokyo a visit for the 1964 Olympics. At this time Japan was still recovering; so while the infrastructure of the capital may have appeared sound, it was quite a different situation in the smaller cities and towns across the nation. Moreover, the first generation of Japanese who knew nothing of their country having an imperial ideology was coming of age. As the 'baby boomers', born between 1947-1949, responded to the national fervor which promulgated that education was a vehicle for social mobility, the sons of farmers traded-in their *jikatabi* (two-toed rubber boots) and *minokasa* (straw-wicker hats) for the sleek business suit and briefcase of a salary-man. This marked Japan's first post-war period of rapid economic growth: a stretch which lasted until the Oil Crisis in 1973. By revising its industrial structure, Japan was able to limit its losses and by the mid-80s the fruit of their labor again took root as the big-wig financial cliques, called *zaibatsu*, merged into modern business conglomerates known as *keiretsu*. This development produced the economic miracle known as the "Bubble Economy." Regarded as a contemporary marvel, the tremendous economic growth of Japan throughout the postwar years has been both venerated and vilified by the western media who dubbed the *keiretsu* conglomerates "Japan Inc." because they received support from the government. This occurred in the late 1980s, just prior to the Nikkei stock soaring to an all-time high in '89 only to crash in spectacular fashion—and with it the real estate bubble collapsed, creating a period of severe financial stagnation which economists have labeled as the "Lost Decades."

Since the Bubble Economy of the 1980s, western trends in fashion and music, not to mention motifs like fast-food restaurants and convenience stores, have become ubiquitous icons. That said, dwarfing any of the Japanese government's efforts to internationalize its citizens is the decision by M.E.X.T., the Ministry of Education, Culture, Sports, Science and Technology (文部科学省), to make English-study a compulsory subject. In spite of the government's strong encouragement, it is questionable as to whether or not the average Japanese embraces the idea of studying the so-called 'International Language.' And when you think about it, how could it be any other way? I mean, how would you feel if you were *forced* to learn a foreign language? And let's not forget we're talking about the tongue of the people who conquered their country in the not-so-distant-past. So it should come as no surprise that Japanese—their affinity for demonstrating xenophobia aside—would develop a psychological method to defend their right to live as they see fit and, in many cases, this does not include anything outside of their own culture.

Understanding the Complex

In psychology, a complex is a system of interrelated, emotion-charged ideas, feelings, memories, and impulses that, due to being repressed, gives rise to abnormal or pathological tendencies. Considering the excessively catastrophic circumstances surrounding how Japan lost World War II—what *Dave Chappelle* described as "having the masculinity bombed out of them"—isn't it only natural that Japanese have sustained in their collective psyche some sort of complex? Following the complete annihilation of their home, many have forgotten how for the next six-plus years these self-proclaimed descendants of the (superior) *Yamato* race were then publicly humiliated by being confined in isolation with General MacArthur and his S.C.A.P. Occupation Force. The author of *Embracing Defeat: Japan in the Wake of World War II*, John W. Dower, describes this imprisoned period as: "an almost sensual embrace with its American conquerors."

What are the psychological ramifications of being defeated in such a vile manner? And then to right-away be forced to not only cohabitate with the enemy but, in addition, to embrace their customs and language? The trauma of being force-fed western ideas, such as the 'humanizing' of the Emperor, has left its mark on the Japanese psyche when it comes to confronting anyone or anything from the West (欧米). Understanding how the unconscious tendencies of Japanese reveal their true feelings as opposed to their publicly displayed opinion, it becomes easy to discern the symptoms of their post-traumatic stress disorder. In society, perhaps the most pervasive embodiment of this complex is the *Eigo-Hoe*.

Chapter 3: Eigo-Hoe

Eigo (英語) is Japanese for the English language. A *hoe* is a common farming tool used to remove weeds from fields. Since this device gets used over and over again by just about any field-hand, in the black community, this word has become synonymous with *whore*. There are both literal and figurative Eigo-hoes so all of them are not necessarily sexually promiscuous. While the literal variety fits both words to a tee, the figurative kind only make use of their English ability, not their bodies. Literal Eigo-Hoes are almost always females. This is not because females are more promiscuous than males but rather it is much easier for women to barter sex (or the possibility/hope of sex) for attention. These women are obsessed with keeping an English-speaking guy by their side. Truth be told, some of these hoes trade guys on such a regular basis, they'll do anything to attract one…*and I do mean anything.* The only stipulation is the guy must be from one of the major English-speaking countries—in some cases black or white does not matter. However if an Asian native-speaker looks too Japanese, I imagine this could hurt his chances. Aside from the constant appearances at British pubs, hip hop clubs, or any westernized function frequented by non-Japanese, their most defining characteristic is their affinity for mixing-up the names of their foreign playmates. Allow me to add this phenomenon knows no boundaries. A friend of mine named Malik, who is a tall, lanky black guy from Chicago, dated an Eigo-hoe for a couple months who would constantly confuse him for her ex-boyfriend. What made this interesting was that her ex, a cool guy named Chad, happened to be a short white guy from somewhere in northern Europe. A few of my friends and I used to share a chuckle every time she would call Malik 'Cha-do' by mistake. *How do you confuse a tall dreadlocked ball player with a short, white-guy sporting a dirty-blonde crew-cut?*

What Eigo-hoes share in common is an unwavering commitment to speak English to Westerners at *all* times—even if the person they are addressing is speaking (fluent) Japanese. Believe it or not, this sometimes even includes people who *cannot* speak English. Back in 2013, I taught an English lesson to a group of eight Japanese girls who were in junior high school. One of the girls had an exchange student from France staying at her home so she brought her to our lesson. Since the French girl's English level was far below that of the Japanese girls', on that evening we just played simple ESL games. At the conclusion of our lesson, all nine girls moved to the far-side of the room while I taught a different group. For the entirety of both lessons, the Japanese girls continually tried to communicate with the French girl in English; this, despite her repeatedly reminding them she could not understand. I will never forget how the French girl finally lost her temper and yelled out: "*Eigo wakaranai!* (I can't understand English!) *Nihongo shabete-kudasai* (Please speak Japanese)." During the 90-minutes leading up to that moment, I heard her say both phrases either separately or together at least ten times. From my perspective, it was mind-boggling watching those Japanese girls continually make the same social gaffe over and over again. It was clear they were not intentionally being rude but, for some reason, their subconscious would not accept that a Caucasian person did not speak English. It was as if their mental-programming refuted the very concept.

J.S.P.E.X. = Japanese Self-Proclaimed English Experts

Japanese who aggressively seek the attention of foreigners have been labeled by the media as "Gaijin Hunters." The most arrogant and pompous of this group are J-Spex. These Figurative Eigo-hoes are extremely proud of their English-speaking ability and, as a result, they constantly invent opportunities to communicate with foreigners. If you happen to encounter a J-Spex at a train station, in a store, or any public area where people congregate, and feel he/she is speaking inordinately loud (in English), you are probably not imagining it. And you're also not crazy. It took me some time to realize that many J-Spex, especially older men, like to showcase their language ability to anyone who happens to be in the vicinity. This is because Japanese who can speak English get props in the society; it is seen as cool. For this reason, please be aware that while in Japan, on the spur-of-a-moment, you may unwittingly be selected to take part in one of these live performances. Since the J-Spex is a 'legend in his own mind', of course, he is the star of these productions. Therefore you get slotted into the side-kick supporting role. Whenever this occurs you may notice the tone used by the man or woman resembles the demeanor of an actor on stage: it seems they are speaking more *at* you, than *to* you. By the third or fourth time of being subjected to this treatment, you may feel more like an English-speaking robot than a human being. To be fair, there are some who are not fanatical about speaking English. However, due to their inherited complex, what these people believe about you and your role in their society is not very different. They just lack the outgoing personality necessary to express themselves. If these lower-level J-Spex are spoken to in Japanese they may reluctantly switch languages. But it is far more common to encounter the extreme variety who, whenever addressing foreigners, *refuse* to speak Japanese.

Over the years I've met some people, mainly exchange students, who have admitted that in order to get locals to speak Japanese they pretend they cannot speak or understand English. Every year, with hundreds of Japanese visiting the U.K., Australia, New Zealand, Canada, as well as the United States for the sole purpose of studying English, why is it so difficult for Japanese to digest the idea of someone coming to their country to learn Japanese? The answer to this riddle was inadvertently revealed while I was working in Kyoto at a private high school. During a team-teaching lesson with a Japanese teacher, while gesturing in my direction, he encouraged the students to *"Steal his language!"* Speaking in Japanese, the man actually used the word 'steal.' He went on to say: "Once you learn English, there is no reason to ever speak Japanese to foreigners." After the lesson, when I explained the numerous reasons why his comments were inappropriate, neither he nor our supervisor seemed to understand. However they did not argue the point and the incident got chalked-up as a misunderstanding. From the off-beat way they tried to play it down, I surmised the ideology of keeping Westerners out—the *sakoku* closed-country mindset—was still in full effect.

The Gaijin Interview

For Japanese who are meeting foreigners for the first time, they are obligated to put the newcomer through a rigorous interrogation. *"Where're you from?"* Whether in Japanese or English, this is always—without exception—the first question. Followed by inquiries concerning the reason you came to Japan and the length of your stay, by this point, if you're nice enough to still be participating in what has now become a full-length investigation, it may then proceed onto more private details about your age, marital status, and even probe the types of girls/guys you're attracted to ("Do you like Japanese girls?") before ending at the finale: "Can you use chopsticks?" and/or "Can you eat natto?" (Never is it: _Do_ you eat natto?) The final questions have a dual purpose. In addition to discussing the complexities of eating with wooden sticks or how nasty fermented soybean paste may or may not taste, it is easy to share a laugh together. This distracts the interviewee of any consideration that he/she has been verbally violated, thereby assuring harmonious relations for the remainder of the encounter.

Only in Japan is it normal protocol to discard routine etiquette when dealing with the foreign population. Why do so many Japanese feel comfortable to stare, alienate, or fire consecutive questions at a total stranger, but never with their own countrymen? Since expressing the real thoughts in their heart (_honne)_ is taboo, Japanese conceal their desire to be confrontational with subtle gestures and indirect tendencies. Their repetitive use of the word 'foreigner' demonstrates this inclination as it illustrates their veiled xenophobia. Having witnessed hundreds, if not thousands, of these gaijin inquisitions—not to mention being the victim of my share—it still amazes me how these proceedings are tolerated to the point where once the Japanese inquisitor has amused himself to his satisfaction, the conversation either moves to a completely different subject or it ends without any type of cross-examination whatsoever. In most cases, the Japanese interviewer is rarely asked to divulge much more personal information than their first name and perhaps their hometown. The fact that *every* Japanese person's number-one priority in *every* chance-encounter with non-Japanese is to impose this questionnaire—in virtually the same order—suggests this behavior is not an expression of free-will but, instead, a symptom of a learned complex. In chapter 12, we will discuss how to appropriately respond to Gaijin Interviews.

Chapter 4: Gaijin History

In 1494, Pope Alexander VI divided the world in half in accordance with the Treaty of Tordesillas, bestowing the western regions onto Spain and the eastern to Portugal. By the 1540s, Christian missionaries began arriving to Japan with Francis Xavier and the Jesuit Order. Aside from their primary objective, which was to persuade people to switch their spiritual allegiance from the Emperor and their Japanese ancestors to the Pope and Jesus Christ, perhaps their most notable attribute was their uncleanliness. It was just over a hundred years prior, during the 14th century, when "The Plague" ravaged Europe, killing more than half of its population. In this regard, their lack of personal hygiene among other peculiar cultural habits, such as eating meat so raw it was dripping blood, prompted the need for new terminology to describe these never-seen-before debased customs. Gaijin or the "Southern Barbarian" was the 'new type of foreigner' who sailed to Japan from the South. In addition to the characteristics already mentioned, this outlander was considered more barbaric than the Emishi, Ainu, or other Asians because they were unable to master the use of chopsticks, and this was believed to be a characteristic of civilized human beings. Even today, this notion of Westerners not possessing the dexterity to use chopsticks still persists. If you don't believe me, just ask any non-Asian person who has visited Japan how many times Japanese paid them a compliment on their ability to use *o-hashi* (chopsticks). Note: This occurs whether the person is extremely skilled or cannot use them at all.

Due to both of my parents being ostracized by their families for marrying outside their race, I never met my grandparents. Like many in need, however, I was fortunate to have others who stepped in to fill the void. One such man, who I revere as a 'grand-uncle', told me as a boy: "Never accept being called a Gaijin." According to him it was okay for whites to be labeled because in his own words: "Those bastards dropped atomic bombs on Japan—but not on Germany!" I always discourage blacks from referring to themselves as gaijin. Many people have been indoctrinated with the erroneous idea that gaijin (外人) simply means foreigner and that, furthermore, 'Gaijin' and 'Gaikokujin' are interchangeable. This is only true if you're referring to the connotation of these words, which means their contemporary usage. But what about the denotation? This is the origin and how and why these words came into existence. In English-Japanese dictionaries 'foreigner' is translated as gaikokujin (外国人); there is no mention of gaijin. According to writer, Yumi Nakata, in her article entitled *Uchi-Soto and Japanese Group Culture*, she identifies Gaikokujin as non-Japanese nationals including other Asians, while Gaijin is a term designated for Caucasians from the West.

Originally, Gaijin only referred to the Portuguese (and later other European) pirates, explorers, missionaries, and merchants who arrived during the Nanban Trade Period (南蛮 貿易時代). Better known as the Southern Barbarian Trade, it commenced with the arrival of Europeans to Japan in 1543 and lasted until 1614. By this time, almost all of them had been evicted or killed under the promulgation of the *Sakoku Seclusion Edicts*. Gaijin became the coined pejorative due to the unusual customs of the Portuguese, Dutch, and Spanish they encountered. Although I do not doubt some of this was also the result of Japanese close-mindedness to foreign culture, it must be noted their savage view of Europeans was largely due to the Jesuit priests teaching that bathing and other forms of personal hygiene were evil. According to the Catholic Church, bathing invited demonic possession, while the accumulation of dirt and sweat repelled these same diabolical forces. In spite of this, there are still some who debate as to whether the Chinese characters for gaijin: gai (外), which means 'outside' and jin (人), which means 'human', denotes a being which exists outside of human civilization—a barbarian—or someone who is simply a foreigner by today's standards. Since westerners, for the most part, do not complain about the designation, 'gaijin' is frequently used in the everyday lexicon. Originally, however, the intrinsic meaning, vibration, and intention behind the word were very similar to that of *Toubob* in Gambia, *Gweilo* in Hong Kong, *Gringo* in Latin America, and *Cracka* or *Honky* in the United States.

Why has Gaijin become ubiquitous?

Following World War II, "Americanism" really began to take off around the globe. At this point, *Neocolonialism*, which focuses on the colonization of a person's mind rather than controlling a foreign country's government and its resources, became the favored policy. During the 1980s, 1990s, and 2000s, although innovative ideas, music, and fashion from the West were continuously introduced, Japanese never stopped using the term. As the notion of Japan being an imperial threat faded from memory and, subsequently, the island in the Far East came to be viewed as an ally of the United States, westerners no longer felt threatened. This resulted in the trend we see nowadays. That said, if you research the origin of this word (as well as the others previously mentioned) you will find this has not always been the case. Since whites have either embraced it or at least do not take offense, many blacks have likewise followed their lead, claiming they don't mind being called gaijin either. This notwithstanding, what is not being mentioned is a complex shared by many blacks that compels them to associate being grouped with whites as a 'come up' in society: a sort of promotion. Let's face it, not only blacks but many so-called minorities are *tickled pink* to be associated with Europeans. At the mere thought of their new 'whitened' classification some folks cannot stop themselves from getting goose-bumps. This sentiment, however, does not necessarily extend to all immigrants, especially those from Asian countries like China or South Korea.

Not for Gaijin

This disclaimer means exactly what it is written. Please do not confuse this with the narrow-minded view of gaijin not being welcome to read this book. Nor does it mean they will not be able to grasp anything useful. It is my hope that anyone who reads it will learn something valuable for their life in Japan. However, please keep in mind, I am specifically addressing the needs and concerns of a certain group of people; so if something does not resonate with you—whether you're Black, White, Asian, Arab, or Latino—it is probably because you have the mindset of a gaijin. Allow me to mention that very few people understand how the term came into existence and most non-Japanese do not mind being called gaijin. As a result, it is natural for Japanese to use it.

To those who disagree with the idea of the denotation of gaijin (or any of the aforementioned pejoratives) solely referring to Europeans, I encourage you to use common sense and think of the number of disparaging words which exclusively indicate specific races. There are boatloads of belittling terms for Blacks *only*, Latinos *only*, or Asians *only*; but somehow when it comes to the colonizers of the entire globe, we're supposed to believe that no one ever came up with any not-nice terminology for them only?

Chapter 5: The Prognosis

Western society is composed of three key components: (1) Greco-Roman philosophy and government, (2) the creation and maintenance of (European) nation-states, and of course we cannot forget (3) the religion of Christianity. Japan, likewise, has its own foundational principles which give life to their standard operating procedure: the *Yamato Code*. Since part 3 is devoted to explaining the Code, for now, please understand Japanese start applying pressure on you to conform from the first Gaijin Interview: this is your initiation into their society. By setting the precedent in this relationship of who is doing the asking and who is doing the answering, not to mention the questions are designed for foreigners, they passively establish the understanding that you are NOT Japanese (as if you thought you were). From their perspective, this equivocates to the fact that you are alone, different, and somehow weird, while simultaneously setting in place the mindset that Japanese represent everything that is good, harmonious, and *normal*. Keep in mind the need for Japanese to alienate anyone or anything not deemed Japanese is at the very foundation of their society—i.e. it's the engine that powers the machine. "*Uchi-Soto (inside-outside)* is the key to understanding Japanese society and why Japanese people behave the way they do, and how they view foreigners." Author, Yumi Nakata, explains the core concept is "based on dividing people into two groups." Not being recognized as a member of the 'in-group' is akin to being cast into a state of purgatory. The only exception are short-term visitors. In this case the script is temporarily suspended, resulting in strictly polite treatment; but all other deviants are branded with the scarlet letter of 'different' and treated accordingly. Considering that, by nature, most non-Japanese (especially blacks) look and act differently than Japanese, they are automatically prone to being targeted for alienation. Many remain unaware of how this passive method of alienation, which I call 'otherizing,' is just a variation of *ijime* (bullying), or that it is one of the pillars of Japanese society. This explains why it is not uncommon to discover mixed-race kids, ex-pats, and even exchange-students who suffer from the same trauma symptoms as the victims of bullying.

What is the effect of being subjected to the Japanese Complex on a daily basis? This depends on a person's circumstances. Therefore, in the next section, we will discuss the innermost psyche of many of the black people who decide to settle down in Japan.

Part 2: Introspection

Chapter 6: Black Analysis

As stated in the previous chapter, the degree to which the Japanese Complex affects a person will greatly depend on their individual circumstances. In order to fully understand this intricate topic, I feel it is necessary to acknowledge how much of a toll western colonization has taken on the subconscious of the average black person in Japan. In addition to getting this off my chest, it is vital to emphasize how the effectiveness of this book is contingent on the level of dedication the reader has to claiming her/his humanity. This includes breaking cycles of low self-esteem, naiveté, and ignorance. **Disclaimer:** If you are planning to be in Japan for only a short time, are content with life as a gaijin, or are suffering from self-hatred issues (this includes not being interested in preserving your heritage), much of this may seem irrelevant or unimportant.

Over the years I have lived and worked in various regions of Japan. Due to Japanese having a tendency to lump all non-Japanese into one broad 'foreigner' category, I have found in interactions with students, co-workers, friends, and associates, sooner than later, three details need to be clarified: (1) I am a Black man who is Japanese—not to be confused with a *hafu* or a gaijin. (2) In this day and age of increasing globalization, just because people reside in the same part of the world, or even in the same country, this does not necessarily indicate they share the same culture, values, or religion. And (3) hmm, how should I put it? There is a difference between sovereign-minded Blacks, who exhibit what I like to call 'melanin-richness' in their daily walk-and-talk and, shall we say, compromised blacks who are basically trauma victims who have yet to psychologically overcome the system of racism/white supremacy. This includes the lasting effects of slavery and colonization.

By explaining these three points I establish a precedent which provides the flexibility to bypass stressful conversations which, for the most part, have absolutely nothing to do with me. For example, when Japanese who are familiar with western culture (especially J-Spex) interact with me, many of them think it is natural to discuss whatever Europeans are into such as watching white-sitcoms like *Friends* or *Modern Family*. Sometimes it is the assumption I regularly dine on hamburgers and hot dogs, or celebrate holidays like Thanksgiving or Christmas. Considering how Japan boasts they are a global nation, it is astonishing how uninformed the average person is about anything which occurs outside of their insular society. Put in plainer terms, in this day and age of the Internet, I feel as though Japanese should at least be able to properly stereotype me with questions about *Atlanta* or *Empire* and, instead of Christmas, ask about Kwanzaa— pun intended.

Special Opportunity for Blacks

Similar to many countries, there are numerous pros and cons for living in Japan. People interested in migrating here are, therefore, attracted for a variety of reasons: career opportunities, the low crime rate, a decent healthcare system, or perhaps it is something more visceral like *anime*, the food, or other aspects of the culture. Considering how Japan's native population has been decreasing, coupled with their increasing globalization, there are many employment possibilities for people interested in moving to this island-nation. Nowadays many of the staff in convenience stores and hospitals, including facilities for senior-citizens, are immigrants from the Philippines, Vietnam, Indonesia, and other Asian countries. English-teaching accounts for hundreds of instructors from the United States, England, Canada, as well as Australia and New Zealand. As Japanese acquire a taste for the exotic, restaurants offering authentic Italian, Turkish, or Indian food, have likewise expanded their presence not only in Tokyo, Osaka, and Nagoya, but also in smaller cities and towns, thereby enlarging the need for staff who specialize in these cuisines. And recently, I have been running into entrepreneurs with their own businesses, or those who work at lucrative companies like Mitsubishi and are in supervisory positions. As you can see, the possibilities for those who wish to make a living in Japan, across the board, are endless and only increasing. This being said, it is my belief that black people have the best opportunity of all.

Regardless of the continent or island, it is no secret some of the poorest and most debased communities in the world are those where black people live. *But why is this the situation?* Everyone knows Africa is the continent most plentiful in natural resources. Aside from the billions of dollars generated by mining gold, silver, rubber, oil, and copper, there are precious minerals such as *coltan* which are indispensable for technological devices like computers and cell phones. With all this abundance, why do these African countries remain in poverty? 'A fool and his money are soon parted.' Is this why a mineral-rich nation like the Democratic Republic of the Congo (DRC), which is profusely abundant in coltan, is amongst the poorest countries economically? Is it because the Congolese people or their leaders lack intellect? Although any measurement of intelligence is purely subjective, at least one, the area of academics, might indicate that Africans are anything but slow. Just check the statistics in universities and you will discover the students from the Congo (as well as the entire continent) are at the very top. Furthermore my social-media timeline is constantly flooded with groundbreaking innovations by Kenyans such as engineering student, Roy Alela, who devised a smart-glove technology in 2020 that is capable of converting sign language movements into audio-speech, and intellectual achievements like the 15-year-old Nigerian, Faith Odunsi, who was crowned "Mathematics Queen" in 2021 after defeating high school students from China, England, and the United States in a global competition.

Understanding black people are far from stupid, if we are sincere in our inquiry as to why they cannot rise above the bottom of the socioeconomic ladder, there is but one plausible explanation. There is a concerted, worldwide effort to keep blacks in a state of perpetual servitude. From Adolf Hitler in Nazi Germany, the Ku Klux Klan and COINTELPRO in the United States, and the Apartheid government in South Africa, the documented evidence supporting the existence of a global system of racism/white supremacy is overwhelming. *21st Century Japan Decoded* is written with the assumption the reader is not in denial of this ongoing reality.

Dr. Francis Cress Welsing explains in her book, *The Isis Papers*: "Racism (white supremacy) is the local and global power-system dynamic, structured and maintained by those who classify themselves as white; whether consciously or subconsciously determined; this system consists of patterns of perception, logic, symbol formation, thought, speech, action and emotional response, as conducted simultaneously in all areas of people activity: economics, education, entertainment, labor, law, politics, religion, sex, and war." Notice how she specifically uses the words "those who classify themselves as white." In society, an unwritten rule most people do not like to discuss is the pressure they feel to select between the polarized construct of black versus white. The implication is you must choose a side. If you watch Japanese anime, for example, most of the characters appear to be wide-eyed Caucasians with slightly Asian features. Although Japanese do not want to be European (who are gaijin), if forced to choose between black and white, they definitely are not picking the former. It is my belief, to a certain degree, each and every one of us feel compelled to make this choice. Later, I shall explain my own experience.

So what is the great opportunity?

Japanese have a natural inclination to be wary of anything deemed foreign. Therefore the feeling of being alienated from the populace is an issue facing all immigrants, not just blacks. Moreover, from the perspective of physical safety and emotional stability, since blacks are not threatened on a daily basis by race-soldiers disguised as police officers, and there are few extra benefits for quid-pro-quo acts designed to ingratiate themselves to the western establishment (i.e. *cooning*), in comparison to other developed countries, blacks in Japan are afforded the freedom to live peacefully and be themselves. Simply not being required to 'watch your back' or conform to western standards is enough reason to cheer. This, in fact, corresponds with the 'time to think' mentioned earlier which can possibly germinate into higher levels of cultivation and refinement.

Proud to be Black?

Well are you? Although many people I meet in Japan claim to be proud of their blackness, seldom do I find those whose talk matches their walk. Sovereign Blacks—in their right-state-of-mind—represent the very pinnacle of the human experience. When it comes to natural talent, intelligence, ingenuity, know-how, integrity, morals, ethics, and unconditional love, the original template was forged and tempered on the Mother Continent. Thought of in this way, Africa represents so much more than a land mass because blacks in the Caribbean, the Polynesian islands, or the Americas are no more or less 'African' than the brothers and sisters in Nigeria, Mozambique, or Ghana. We have so much in common and we need to focus on our mutual interests but, at the same time, we also should celebrate what makes us distinct. For Japanese watching the news on NHK, Fuji Television, or even western forms of media like BBC or CNN, it is easy to conclude Africa is not a continent but, rather, an enormously large country that is plagued with war, famine, and corruption. For this reason, in my lessons, I explain how inserting blacks into 'one big African country' has just as slippery a slope as grouping Germans, Brits, and Poles into 'one big European country', or the people in Vietnam, Indonesia, and China into 'one big Asian country.' In Japan, since there is a clear separation between in-groups (*uchi*) and out-groups (*soto*), Japanese have no problem distinguishing native, indigenous populations from white colonizers. However, due to living in a homogeneous society where Koreans, Ainu, Brazilians, as well as other marginalized groups, have been absorbed into the dominant culture, many are surprised to hear it is commonplace in ethnically-diverse countries like the United States to point-out cultural distinctions between Anglo-European, Asian, Latin, Caribbean, and (Foundational) Black Americans. Since I never hesitate to openly discuss discrimination and other topics which might be controversial, such as the growing epidemic of pedophilia or the lucrative prison-industrial complex—from the perspective of a Black person—this alone distinguishes me from other native-language-teachers they have encountered (including other blacks), who basically go along with established western narrative. This is what the ex-NBA player who has recently made a splash in the world of podcasting, Kwame Brown, calls the "go along to get along gang." With this understanding, a couple months ago, I posed a simple question to my melanin-rich brethren who reside in Japan: *Aside from physical characteristics, what distinguishes you from members of other ethnic groups?* If there is nothing about your daily routine that differs from others—especially white people—by definition, can it be said that you're proud of your distinct lineage?

A few years back, I attended a book-fair in Atlanta, Georgia. For those who are unaware, Atlanta is a hub for black intellectuals. While speaking to the attendees who visited my table, I had an interesting conversation with three very educated women. One lady, who held a PhD in Education, more than hinted that I was a 'sell-out' because I lived in Japan. All three women seemed genuinely surprised when, instead of saying nothing or becoming defensive, I wanted to hear more and, for this reason, asked them to explain their supposition. Following a litany of questions about my reasons for living in Japan, my accusers concluded their interrogation with: "You married a Japanese woman, right?"

"Hmm, yeah..." I responded with a grin.

By this time, I had gotten a pretty good idea of their angle, so I suspected this was their coup de grace. In other words they thought they had me on the ropes. They were following the logic that a man (in his right-mind) is naturally attracted to a woman who incorporates the intrinsic traits of his mother. So you can probably imagine it was hard to suppress my laughter when all three of their jaws hit the floor simultaneously once I revealed my mother was Japanese.

"Okay," one of them reluctantly admitted following a lengthy pause, "so maybe *you* are not the Uncle Tom we thought you were." Then another lady completed her thought. "But the rest of those black men who run-off to Japan are straight-up sell-outs!" she emphasized with a finger pointing diagonally upward to indicate somewhere 'over there.'

Until that moment I had never considered some black folks come to Japan mainly in order to distance themselves from other blacks. Therefore I initially thought these women were just old and bitter. That is, until I returned to Japan and started asking blacks to comment on this topic. To my astonishment this line of questioning instantly made some uneasy and even got me ousted from social-media groups— not to mention splintered a few friendships. At this point it became obvious those women's claim had some merit. Let's go deeper: it is often said America is a 'melting pot' of diverse ethnicities and how each of these proud lineages represent their own distinct ideas, culture, values, or religion. And if we examine the lifestyles of several groups who have migrated to the U.S., for example, Jews, Mormons, Indians, Muslims, Amish, etc., we can see some truth to this idea because it is not difficult to ascertain what distinguishes each of these groups from one another as well as from mainstream Catholics or Protestants. So if you, as a black person, only celebrate the same holidays, pray to the same deities, and eat the same food as everyone else, in what manner are you expressing your distinct heritage? My point is that if anyone, regardless of their race, adopts western attitudes, customs, and religions—without reservation—do they not fall into the category of *toubob*, *gringo*, or *gweilo*? We shall discuss these terms in the following chapter and demonstrate how they correspond to gaijin but, for the time being, please understand that aside from your phenotype or some other surface characteristic, if there is very little to distinguish you from a white person, this is perfectly okay. However, in order to stay in touch with reality, some sort of distinction must be made.

Chapter 7: Frequency & Vibration

Throughout my life, I've had the opportunity to have extended stays in more than a few countries. In my travels to Jamaica, the Dominican Republic, and even Gambia, I've found that outside of the tourist areas how I was treated had less to do with my physical appearance, as more attention was directed toward my *frequency* and *vibration*. Put simply, people of those countries were keen to evaluate my intrinsic qualities instead of surface-level characteristics like the color of my skin or passport. Not every time—but more times than not—I've discovered that although I might arrive to a country as a *gringo* or *toubob*, soon thereafter, the locals stop using those demeaning terms. Allow me to share a few examples to illustrate my point.

The Dominican Republic

I had a co-worker in New Brunswick, New Jersey who was Dominican. His name is Hilario and we became good friends. After a year-and-a-half of eating *arroz con pollo*, *platanos*, or just beans and rice at his parent's house, not to mention learning how to dance *merengue*, *salsa*, and *bachata* at Latin-American functions, Hilario persuaded me to accompany him on a trip to the Dominican Republic. For the majority of our stay, we resided with his relatives in San Jose de la Matas, which is a small town in the province of Santiago. During the first couple of days, I remember hearing the word *gringo* being mentioned in reference to me; but within a week, they started calling me *Negro*. A few days later, this pseudonym was again changed to *Moreno* which, by the way it was uttered, seemed to be some sort of upgrade. And, believe it or not, from there I made myself so at home that, by the time I arrived at the airport some weeks later, an official at the airport accused me of being a Dominican with a fake passport. He actually thought I was trying to sneak into the United States! *This does not happen to gringos!* Due to the fact that, to a certain degree, I phenotypically resemble a Dominican someone might attempt to chalk this mix-up to being nothing more than my physical appearance. But I'm telling you this was not the case. It goes much deeper.

By now you may be asking yourself: what is the point of elaborating on this experience? The answer is to ascertain why it might be logical for Japanese to label you as 'gaijin.' This goes beyond merely being a foreigner; it is also associated with how you move, talk, think, and express yourself. If your talking-points mirror white folks' and you, yourself, identify as a 'gaijin' then it is only natural for Japanese to likewise treat you as a descendant of the very same people who dropped atomic bombs on their nation—i.e. an invading colonizer. For those who are not convinced, please allow me to explain another such time when something similar to my experience in the Dominican Republic occurred. And, in this case, I did not resemble the native population at all. This occurred on the other side of the planet in Mother Africa.

Gambia

Ironically, it was during a 3-week stay in Gambia when I really became convinced that 'gaijin' and most derogatory terms associated with foreigners had nothing to do with black people. By the time I visited Gambia, which is in West Africa, I had been living in Japan for about five years. Right away, I noticed how the Gambian employees at the hotel, mostly young men, went out of their way to address me either as *toubob* or boss man. Now, in the United States, some blacks may say 'boss' as a slang-term of endearment similar to 'man' or 'brother'; for example "What's up boss?" For this reason, at first, I was not sure as to the meaning of either term. However, after a day or so, when I saw them referring to white guests the same way, I realized they were casually lumping me into the same category with white people—just like how Japanese put Arabs, Blacks, and Indians in the same group as Europeans and call them 'gaijin.' Having made this assessment, in a friendly manner, I confronted a group of five or six employees on the subject. "This word *toubob*," I said scratching my chin, "what does it mean?" My inquiry brought instant grins to their faces as they innocently responded it only meant something akin to 'friend.' In spite of their benign reply, by the way they were grinning and laughing the entire time, it was clear they were making fun of me; they were not even putting any effort into being convincing. The next day none of them seemed to remember the discussion from the previous night. But I did. I repeatedly referred to the employees as both *toubob* and boss man in a casual, friendly manner. Initially, this only made them laugh even harder than the night before. Nonetheless I noticed their amusement was a bit toned-down whenever I did it in the lobby, or in the presence of any Gambians they did not know. In other words they were uncomfortable if Gambians who were not privy to the discussion from the previous evening—anyone not in on the joke—heard me calling them *toubob*. You should have seen the disgruntled looks on their faces; I regret not taking photographs.

Long-story-short, not only did they eventually admit these terms did, indeed, refer to the colonizer of their lands, when I was checking-out of the hotel a few weeks later, four of the employees who were involved in this social experiment came to my door, unsummoned, and volunteered to carry our luggage to the taxi. Before I could respond they emphasized they did not want any money for the courtesy-service. Hearing them say they would not accept a tip certainly got my attention. For those who have never visited a so-called developing country, especially one in Africa, you may be missing the enormity of this phenomenon because I cannot stress how much hustling tourists for chump-change is a full-time occupation.

As we walked through the open-air common area, the senior member of the group pointed at a few of the (white) guests who were seated with hotel staff on two separate benches along the walkway. Both groups seemed to be involved in lively discussions. Not seeing anything worthy of comment, I looked back toward the manager in silence. "I've been working here for twelve years," he began, seeming to understand my cluelessness. "These *toubob* have never talked to us in a friendly way like this until they saw you doing it." Saying this, he continued to gesture back and forth at the two ongoing conversations. "After they saw you hanging-out with us night after night," he reiterated, "they started copying you." As I digested the weight of his words, we exited the hotel and arrived at a parked taxi. Switching to his native Fulani dialect, he greeted the cabbie before telling his staff to load the bags into the trunk. Once my suitcases were in the cab, I hugged each staff member before the manager resumed his explanation about why they would not accept a tip. "You don't behave like a hotel guest, he said while still shaking my hand. "What I mean is, I've never met a guest like you." Realizing his point was not getting across, he continued. "Yes, of course, you were our guest but even when a person's relatives travel to their home from another district they, too, are guests, right? But no one expects a tip from their grannie, or their uncle or aunt; that is unthinkable." As I was about to reply he spoke again. "Whenever you were at the hotel, you hung out with us and treated everyone like a brother." Then he referred to a new group of arriving guests who were exiting a shuttle-van from the airport. The group consisted of mostly whites but there were a few dark-skinned tourists peppered-in amongst them. "Before you came, the only time they spoke to us was when they were asking for directions, or when they needed us to carry something." Then he chuckled before adding, "Thanks to you, maybe from now on, our job description might include having conversations with *toubob*." As everyone shared a laugh another member of the group, a younger guy who I had especially hit it off with, summed up the manager's words: "Brother Tak," he said pointing at me, "you are not a *toubob* or a boss man…you are our brother!"

Had I caught it on film, the confused look on the cabbie's face would have been another classic photo.

Gaijin Test

It never fails to make me laugh whenever Japanese return from their initial business trip or vacation overseas and exclaim in a moment of exuberance: "This was the first time I have ever seen so many *gaijin* in one place!" I have a tendency, however, to ruin the moment by following up this statement with: "But wait a minute, I thought gaijin meant 'foreigner?' So in this case *you* were the gaijin, right?"

Realizing they went off-code, they usually offer a crooked smile in reply along with a weak nod and an almost inaudible "*hai.*" Throughout the years, I have conducted what I call the 'Gaijin Test' several times. In fact, I just conducted one last week with my newest student, who happens to be a 42-year-old tax accountant. After having her close her eyes, I told her (in Japanese) to imagine this situation: "Yesterday, at the train station, you saw a family consisting of four gaijin." Now, without any more explanation, I asked her to describe the image in her mind. This woman who, just minutes before, had disagreed with my claim that the real meaning of gaijin exclusively identifies Caucasians, promptly stated what *all* Japanese imagine in regards to the appearance of typical gaijin. She described the four people at the station as having blonde (brown or red) hair, big, round, blue eyes, and pale (white) skin. Now, as we all know, this is a far cry from any depiction of black people. In fact, her description brings to mind how perhaps the most infamous person in recent history, Adolf Hitler, identified his so-called "master race." So, at the end of the day, I am convinced the denotation of pejoratives like gaijin, *toubob*, *gringo*, or *gweilo* have as much to do with black people as the man on the moon.

Black, White, or 'Hafu'?

"Life is not black and white but a million shades of grey"

Catchy saying but is it true? I ask this simply because if we take just a cursory peek at the 'real world' we see almost nothing but examples of dichotomous constructs. Democrats vs. Republicans, right-wing vs. left-wing, liberals vs. conservatives, Crips vs. Bloods, Tupac vs. Biggie, Lebron vs. MJ. Let's face it, this is how people have been programmed to think. Take, for instance, the last comparison mentioned about basketball's G.O.A.T. (Greatest of All Time). Maybe you think the all-time king of the hardwood is someone else. But even if you believe the best-player-ever is Kareem Abdul-Jabbar, Bill Russell, or even Kobe Bryant, chances are you will then pit your favorite player against one of the other players on the list to create a different one-on-one scenario. For example: Kobe vs. MJ. But considering the endless number of great phenoms who have come and gone, shouldn't the conversation include more players? Surely, in addition to the stars already mentioned, there are others who have the credentials for supreme greatness. What about Magic, Oscar Robertson, or Wilt Chamberlain? My point is, it matters little whether this way of thinking is something that has been engineered by the media / government, or nothing conspiratorial or diabolical at all. What matters is, thinking in dual terms is a result of living in the 21st century, and it is undeniable that society demands we view everything the world has to offer in terms of good vs. evil.

In book 1 of *Gaikokujin – The Story*, I recall my initial encounter with feeling pressure to choose a racial designation: either black or white. I remember thinking it was strange. For many children, due to being immersed in a homogeneous culture since birth, this decision is a no-brainer. However this is not true for all children, especially those from multiethnic backgrounds. Some people may be surprised to hear that I believe everyone around the world is affected. For those who doubt the veracity of this statement, how then do you explain the overabundance of 'whitening cream' in India, the Philippines, or various African countries? Or how about a black person being dubbed "a sell-out", an "Uncle Tom" or an "Oreo"? An Asian being called a "Twinkie" or a

"Banana"? Or, at the other end of the spectrum, what about the white (or Asian) person who is labeled a "Nigger Lover"? To be clear, I do not in any way, shape, or form endorse such thinking; I only acknowledge its existence. Having said that, *21st Century Japan Decoded* is written in black and white, not shades of gray. Furthermore it was created for Black people. In all honesty, it is about staying in my lane: in other words this book was written by a Black person who is also Japanese. Please do not confuse me with someone who is half-black, part-Japanese, or anything which implies less than whole. No disrespect to anyone who identifies or uses terms like *Hafu*, *Hapa*, or *Blasian* but, for me, excluding the phrase "half man-half amazing" (shout-out to Nas!), I would never consider identifying as half of, or less than, anyone or anything. Aside from the self-deprecation embedded, more importantly, where is the logic? I say this because I am a member of more than one culture—as opposed to being half of one and half of another. As a child, I never understood how a person could be only half of a race (or culture) but not the other half. Furthermore, in terms of DNA, how can this be explained? So, whether culturally or scientifically speaking, it never added up.

But now I understand.

I used to debate the foolish idea of people being 'half' until I began to study different levels of human development. Just as an adolescent is more developed and, therefore, physically stronger than an infant but, at the same time, less-developed and weaker than an adult, this is also true along the mental and spiritual planes. So instead of trying to convince people that 50% of anything is equivalent to failure, I learned to look into these personalities to see why they view themselves this way. While dissecting this concept, it became obvious how, to Japanese, whether a person is American, Korean, Canadian, Nigerian, German, or even *hafu*, it just means they are not Japanese. This is their form of duality. In their minds Japan is the center of the universe and, for this reason, there are only two types of people: those who are 100% Japanese and those who are not.

Nonetheless, upon further evaluation, I would argue the rigidness of Japanese society has unwittingly created not two, but three designations. Inserted between Japanese and gaijin are the *Gaikokujin*. These are the (self-respecting) foreign-nationals mentioned earlier which include, but are not limited to, other Asians. In contrast, if we examine another unbending society from the not-so-distant-past that likewise promoted strict racial classification, the South African Apartheid system, we also see three distinct groups: White, Colored, and Black-African. Although the two systems have similarities, one major difference is the function of the middle group. In South Africa, the colored-group was intentionally created by the government to serve as a sort of 'buffer class' between the white oppressors and the downtrodden blacks who comprised the majority of the population. The colonizers, being woefully outnumbered, realized the need to create division among the disenfranchised in order to deflect attention away from them and onto each other. By lending the mixed-blacks and other lighter-complexioned people a few more benefits than the darker-skinned folks, this naturally fueled vitriol and jealousy between the lower groups. The demographics of Japan, however, are different. Considering that, unlike the *Afrikaans*, Yamato-Japanese comprise the overwhelming majority, they have no need for buffers. For this reason it would be more accurate to define the middle classification in the Japanese system as certain individuals, not necessarily a group. These people have attained an awareness of not only how Japanese function but also of themselves. It is this understanding which allows them to transcend the lifestyle of a lowly gaijin.

Fully grasping this dynamic and its implications, in my opinion, is the key to standing your ground in a pressurized society in which interpersonal affairs between individuals (*sempai-kohai*), as well as a single person to the larger group, are fixed and unmoving. In such a conservative environment, learning how to 'save face' in any situation is vital for survival; but this is only possible for those who have attained mastery of themselves, including their emotions. This is because, at the end of the day, how well you are able to project your image—by Japanese standards—is going to determine what level of respect you garner from co-workers, associates, and whoever else you interact with on a regular basis. And please never forget, in Japan, the group-mentality dominates everything.

Chapter 8: Out of your Mind

"If you do not understand white supremacy/racism—what it is and how it works— everything else that you do understand, will only confuse you."~Dr. Neely Fuller Jr.

So I already explained this book is written for black people…but not just any black person. Allow me to explain. In 2022, this should be common knowledge by now but I'll say it anyway: the average black person is out of their mind. We often dismiss people who are "out of their mind" as meaning they are simply insane or crazy but, in this case, that is not exactly what I mean. I am literally saying many black people, despite the darkness of their complexion or the coiled texture of their afro, function almost completely outside of a black person's natural mind. Instead, they've been programmed through generations of repetitious trauma and negative imagery to devalue their blackness and, as a result, attempt to attach themselves to anything which does not remind them of being black: i.e. the Republican Party, the LGBTQ+, white people, or perhaps another ethnic group. Many blacks have devolved to the point they do not mind second-class citizenship, so long as they can rationalize their superiority over the average black person. I've already mentioned how a few months ago, in face-to-face interactions as well as via social media, I challenged blacks with a question. "Aside from physical characteristics, what distinguishes you from people in other ethnic groups?" Something worth mentioning is that my social network primarily consists of two platforms and both are related to black people: conscious groups and folks living in Japan. As the replies came in I noticed a strict divide in the responses.

On one hand, the conscious brothers and sisters had no difficulty telling me about their Dr. Sebi diet, their connection to *Ogun, Yemenya, Shango*, or other African-based spiritual systems. Some mentioned performing daily rituals which included meditation or yoga. One brother talked about his 'swag' or demeanor, and how he was raised in the (original) culture of Hip Hop. A few sisters went-in on how they possessed the inner-strength of a Sojourner Truth, a Harriet Tubman, or a Winnie Mandela. What these responses have in common is the ability to go inward and identify a melanin-rich attribute within themselves which they project to the outside world. Basically any intrinsic characteristic would qualify. That is, if the respondent was truly proud to be black.

This was in direct contrast with the sites for black people living in Japan. Of the twenty or so comments I read, none of the respondents were able to come up with anything beyond the surface (i.e. physical) level. Many seemed to have difficulty with just understanding the question. The most common responses were related to their 'natural' hair, fashion, or "black girl magic." Now, to me, black girl magic refers to an intrinsic, melanin-rich quality. After all, if you take 'girl' out of the phrase it's 'black magic.' However when I asked one young lady to provide more detail, she started talking about her hair and skin tone. This confirmed something I had suspected for some time: not only is the average black person who resides in Japan out of their mind, many do not even understand what it means to be black. Essentially they are spiritually-bankrupt. In this context, here is another question worth considering: Assuming a black person no longer possesses her/his own mind or spirit, whose thoughts are being processed in their head? Or conversely, who or what is controlling them? This inquiry brings us back to the duality of 'black is bad' and 'white is right' given how blacks adopting the views, attitudes, and values of Westerners has been cited as an example of *Stockholm syndrome*. Defined as a condition in which hostages develop a psychological alliance with their captors during captivity, the emotional bonds between captor and captives created during their intimate time together are generally considered irrational in light of the danger or risk endured by the captives. According to Dr. Joy Degruy: "It is not uncommon for people being held captive to take on the views and attitudes of their captors. At times, under the stressful conditions associated with being held captive, people can identify so closely with their tormentors they become like them… One of the most insidious and pervasive symptoms of Post Traumatic Slave Syndrome (P.T.S.S.) is our adoption of the slave master's value system… Through the centuries of slavery and the decades of institutionalized oppression that followed, many African Americans have, in essence, been socialized to be something akin to white racists. Many have adopted the attitudes and views of white, racist America."

Although her book, *Post Traumatic Slave Syndrome*, is written about blacks in the United States, it is fair to say this mentality spans the entire African diaspora and certainly affects the blacks I meet in Japan. Allow me to summarize in plain English. Many almond-complexioned people see their darker hue through a western lens which results in unconsciously having a negative self-image. Consequently, they believe their inherent qualities, including their ancestor's customs and ways of thinking, are old and outdated—if not outright evil. It is easy to determine where you stand on this issue by giving yourself a simple evaluation. Do you see western society as being intrinsically better than your own?

Are white people somehow closer to God? For more on this concept, please check out the work of Dr. Joy Degruy, Dr. Neely Fuller Jr., or Dr. Francis Cress Welsing.

Land of Broken & Misfit Toys

"Disappear, vamoose, they're wack to me, take them folks back to the factory..."

~Rendition of *Biggie*'s lyrics from the *Flava in ya Ear* remix

There was a Christmas special which used to air every year in the United States back in the 1970s. The story took place on a weird island where all the toys that children did not want were deposited. In the anime, the toys were sentient beings and, therefore, were consciously aware of whatever strange quirk they possessed that made them unappealing to children. For example, there was an airplane that could not fly, a boat that did not float, and a "Charlie-in-the-box" instead of Jack-in-the-box. One quirk I sense in the character of many of the foreign-nationals living in Japan is having a passive nature—which really is not a flaw, per-se. However in western developed countries—especially in the business sector—the ability to assert yourself amongst colleagues and supervisors along with knowing how to take the initiative are both indispensable components of success. This is substantiated by the adage: "Nice guys finish last." Well, many of the foreign-nationals I have met in Japan are far from the ambitious 'go-getter' type and, as a result, are not interested in competing for high-status / salary in their home-countries.

People come in many shapes, sizes, and colors. The limits and possibilities of human development are, therefore, endless. For this reason I find it somewhat perplexing that virtually every person of color I come across in Japan is extremely passive. So what's wrong with being passive? Absolutely nothing at all. If everyone in a society, or even most people, possessed exclusively dominant personalities (i.e. alpha) this would result in just as much imbalance—only on the other side of the spectrum. This would be akin to an indigenous tribe consisting of "All Chiefs and no Indians." The key is balance. Being an alpha male or female does not mean a person does not possess any passive (beta) traits. We can see the same concept being played out in the gender principle of humans and some animals. Within both genders, male and female, is the ability to produce testosterone as well as estrogen. However, in males, since estrogen (the female hormone) is in lesser amounts than testosterone, this explains why most males are attracted to females: i.e. opposites attract. Thus it is only natural that males and females would seek the other side of themselves; this, in order to become whole, or 100%. Any healthy, living organism on this plane of existence is, in their own way, seeking to find that which complements them. This, alone, is enough reason for me to abhor being labeled a "half-breed" no matter the colorful epithet or package in which it is disguised. For blacks in Japan, the reason why the beta-personality is so plentiful can easily be ascertained by understanding why many of them came to Japan.

The overwhelming majority I meet are in entertainment or education; and qualifying at the entry-level of either of these industries is so easy that almost any foreigner can land a gig. This is not to say most of the entertainers or teachers are incompetent but, let's face it, even when a night-club or school has an excellent musician or instructor, a person with only half of his or her ability/experience may qualify for the job. With such low standards in place Japan has become a haven for those who cannot 'cut the mustard' in their own country. In addition, anime-lovers and video game aficionados are also in abundance and these endeavors, by nature, are related to what Japanese call *Otaku*—and these people are ridiculed for being excessively weak, passive, and weird. And we cannot forget Japanese professional sports. Have you ever met a 'blue-chip' athlete in person? Of course there are exceptions to the rule but, by and large, they have huge egos. And why not? After all they train hard, command huge salaries, and are constantly reminded by fans as well as the press about how great they are. In any international sport, to be recognized as the best, it is necessary to compete against the top-tier jocks around the world who lay claim to greatness (i.e. MLB, NBA, Premier League, etc.). For this reason, in order for the Japanese professional leagues to maintain a level of legitimacy, they are forced to recruit a quota of players from overseas. For their sacrifice, a few of these foreign players are lavishly compensated on the financial end; but for the rest of them—which constitutes the majority—playing professional sports in Japan pretty much indicates they are either washed-up or never had what it takes in the first place. All of this results in far too much passive energy.

This conversation would not be complete without mentioning the opportunists from developing countries who are hustling for a marriage visa. Over the years, I have encountered dozens of brothers (and even a few sisters) from the Caribbean islands and the African continent who openly admit they got married to escape the impoverished conditions at home. Some of these folks have multiple family units spanning the globe! Combining the desperation of fleeing poverty with the 'love' shared between a man and a woman creates a dynamic so complex anything can happen so I am hesitant to make a blanket statement regarding these types of affairs. After all desperate times call for desperate measures and, generally speaking, I respect anyone who is doing what they feel needs to be done in order to survive. That being said, for the Africans who tell lies about being from the United States because they believe Japanese women prefer Americans, or the men who become so comfortable impregnating and shacking up with women who pay the bills and, while their 'wives' are at work, they spend their time running the streets with other women, I'm sorry but these toxic, beta-personalities need to be called out.

Ever since childhood, my misfit quality has been an insecurity regarding my mixed-race status. In my youth, I was frustrated because no matter where we lived the societal standards never matched the perception I had of myself. Most people are not surprised to hear that Japanese told me I was not Japanese; but I see more than a few raised eyebrows whenever I reveal how black kids were no less vigilant in letting me know I was not on the black-vibe either. This led me on a quest to find out what it meant to 'be black.' Having overcome that hurdle, the same insecurity eventually drew me, as a young adult, back to Japan to examine the idea of my also 'being Japanese.' At first, I made most of the gaijin mistakes mentioned in this book. Stupidity such as trying to behave in a Japanese manner more than the next foreigner. This may include showing-off your language skills or knowledge of something traditionally Japanese like karate, the Tea Ceremony or *Ikebana* (flower arranging). Put simply, if you are trying to impress people—whether they are Japanese or not—with how Japanese you are for the sole purpose of creating a space which is closer to Japanese than the next foreigner, sooner or later, you're going to fall flat on your face. Yes, it is true you must create your own space; however the space created must be authentically yours. This means it is not some surface-level illusion that, in the long-run, you cannot maintain. Learning how to create space and build a dignified square to stand on is the theme of this book.

Chapter 9: Why the Emphasis on Melanin?

Quite simply because only melanin-rich people will be able to 'get it.' Put another way: for the sake of understanding and implementing the techniques explained later, it will be necessary for the reader to access higher frequencies of their consciousness. Most people regard melanin as either a dark pigment in their skin which provides protection from ultra-violet rays or a pill called melatonin, which puts them to sleep. Although both ideas are technically correct, the study of melanin goes far beyond these shallow attributes.

An indispensable component to living organisms, melanin has been described by lofty phrases such as the "God particle" or "the Key Chemical for Life." In addition to a natural sunblock, people are supposed to have access to other benefits as well such as *neuro-melanin* or *inner-ear melanin*. Unfortunately everyone is not afforded the deeper wonders of this substance. According to Dr. Richard King, this is due to having a calcified pineal gland. Have you ever wondered why some people cannot dance? Why do they lack the ability to rhythmically translate musical-tempo into an expression of bodily movement? Another enigma is people who are devoid of human compassion. An example of this was the police officers who casually kneeled on George Floyd while protesters verbally lambasted them from the sidelines for their inhumane actions. If I had not seen the news footage for myself, it would have been difficult to believe it was possible for human beings to be so cold-blooded. For nearly nine minutes Derek Chauvin slowly crushed a helpless man's windpipe—*with both hands in his pockets!*

There are several reasons for the increasing rate of calcified pineal glands, such as the chemically-laced foods being eaten, lack of sunshine, not to mention the toxins in the air and water but, for blacks, perhaps the number one culprit is stress. Now it is true stress affects everyone regardless of ethnicity, social class, or religion but due to their marginalized status the pressure on blacks is the extremely severe. Japanese, on the other hand, also have a distinctive type of stress which has been tailor-made by their society. Much of this pressure negatively manifests as *hikikomori* (hermitage), *karoshi* (death from overworking), and *jisatsu* (suicide). We also cannot forget nor discount Japan's own historical victims of racism such as the Ainu, Emishi, Ryukyuan, and Burakumin who, in their own right, have a stormy history with discriminatory practices. While searching for a safe space in Japan amid this civilized-barbarity, I was led to a virtually uninhabited zone which could be described as an 'eye' between the storms. Considering I am both Black and Japanese, it was only natural to seek some sort of loophole which might exist between two unrelated systems that equally cast me in a negative light. I feel 'eye between the storms' is an appropriate phrase because, in addition to diminishing the foreigner-target on my back, this state of mind allows me to avoid less-than-pleasant situations by identifying them far in advance. Or, in a worst-case-scenario, it provides the fortitude to stomp problems in their tracks.

Ignorance is Bliss

Each ethnic group and religion has a set of morals, principles, and behavior that reflect their distinct world view. Most Asian countries prefer bows to western-styled handshakes and eating with chopsticks rather than silverware. An adherent of the Jewish faith is required to eat a kosher diet much in the same way that Muslims are prohibited from eating pork. Japanese, Europeans, Arabs, Indians, Jews—*everyone except blacks*—live by a code. Nevertheless just because blacks don't have their own code does not mean they are not following one. The question is: is the code to which they show allegiance one that has been laid-out for *them* to achieve greatness? Or someone else? In spite of the fact that every ethnicity and religious group has a set of values which sets them apart, there are people who scoff at the notion of blacks being on-code with one another. For those who fit this description, why do you think this way? This is an open invitation to challenge yourself. It may be helpful to seek counseling to discuss the deeper, perhaps even hidden-side of your personality. The counselor does not necessarily have to be a practicing psychiatrist or mental-health clinician. Any wise person with life experience and an abundance of common sense, perhaps an older sibling or a life-long friend—someone you trust—is probably a good choice. While we are in this moment of self-contemplation, please take a moment to consider the following. I recommend writing down both the questions and your answers and keeping them in your personal records.

1. According to the definition of gaijin provided earlier, do you (still) consider yourself to be a gaijin? Why? / Why not?
2. What does it mean to be Black? And what distinguishes you as a black person? In other words, what is the difference between you and people of other ethnicities (especially white people)?

3. Who/What is God? This includes spiritual ideology, gender, and a physical description. What is your evidence/proof?
4. Why did you come to Japan? And what led to your deciding to stay? (Be specific)
5. Are you on-code with other blacks? If so, in what way? If not, why not?

Part 3: Land of Yamato

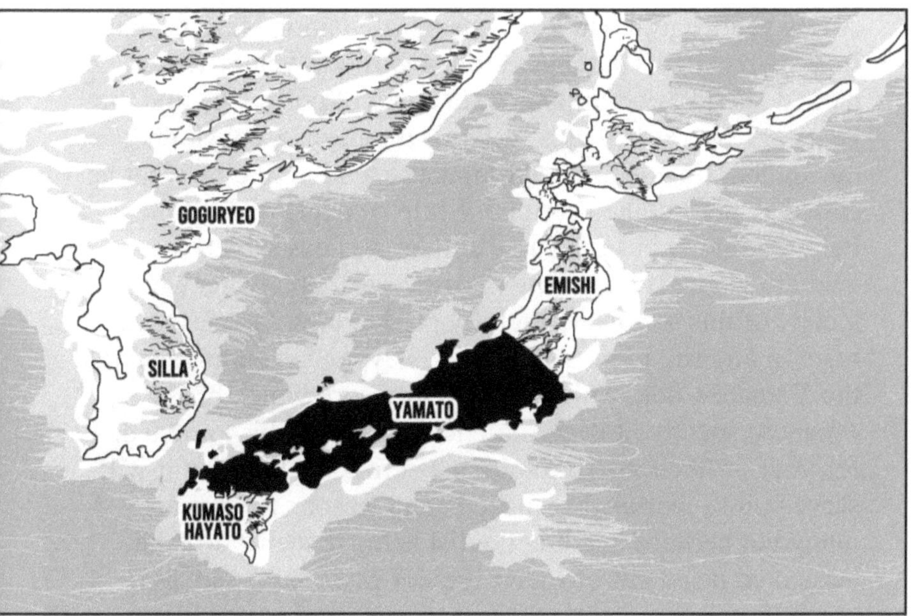

Chapter 10: Yamato Code

A few years ago, I had the pleasure of visiting New Zealand. In a town called Tauranga, I met a world traveler / writer named David Leberknight. Over a cup of coffee, he told me years ago he worked as a systems-engineer in Tokyo and, during that time, he noticed Japanese tend to live by what he called a "preordained script." While he explained his theory a bell rang in my head as I realized he was describing the Yamato Code. If this is true, it suggests that anyone who has a copy of this script can literally predict how Japanese will react in any situation. Put another way, once you understand the Yamato Code, which is the framework which binds Japanese society, it is possible to implement this knowledge for your protection. That said, mastering the Code so it will serve you is challenging indeed. The reasons for this are many but perhaps heading the list is the tendency to take perceived instances of rude behavior personally and, as a result, becoming emotional. If you ever find yourself in a dispute with a Japanese person, the ability to state your case and conduct yourself within the framework of the Code will impact the verdict of innocence or guilt just as much as right or wrong. If you become angry, raise your voice (especially to a higher-ranking person), interrupt by speaking out of turn, or just become too emotional and animated in your delivery—*even if everything you are saying is on-point*—in the eyes of whoever witnesses the spectacle you will almost certainly be the guilty party. And as stated previously, in Japan, the decision of the group overshadows everything.

"For Japanese, being a member of the group is what gives a person his power. The group-dynamic is an energy field

created by the people. This power surrounds us and penetrates us. It binds the society together." ~天流沢庵

Any true *Star Wars* fan should recognize the above quote as a clever reconstruction of *Obi-Wan*'s explanation of "The Force" to a young *Luke Skywalker*. And just like that impenetrable energy-field, in Japan, the power of the group is both omnipresent and omnipotent. Japanese society operates very similar to a hive of bees, a colony of ants, or any organism which exhibits extreme social behavior. Perhaps the best example is how Japanese work in concert to make collective decisions on every short or long-term objective. Anyone who has worked in a Japanese company will attest to how much Japanese love to have meetings! In short, making collective decisions, living up to any obligations incurred in those meetings—which relates to staying on code—as well as contributing to society by working hard and having children, believe it or not, this is the essence of being Japanese…of *Yamato Damashii*.

"Japanese Spirit", "Japanese Soul", "Yamato Spirit", or even "The Soul of Old Japan", these are some of the accepted translations for *Yamato-Damashii* (大和魂). Coined during the Heian Period to juxtapose Japanese cultural values against those of the *Tang Dynasty* (618 to 907) as well as the rest of the Asian continent, the kanji characters literally mean "Spirit of Great Harmony." In the early 20ᵗʰ century, Japanese nationalists propagandized their own translation: "The brave, daring, and indomitable spirit of Japanese people." In spite of its rosy appeal, *Yamato-Damashii* is also mixed with a certain level of pragmatism. In the book, *Group Psychology of the Japanese in Wartime,* Toshio Iritani expresses this in his description of life on the streets of Tokyo during the waning days of WWII. "When people gathered together in groups not a single complaint could be heard and they endured hardship in silence for the sake of their pride. Such reticence stems from 'the Japanese spirit' (*Yamato Damashii*) which, in this writer's opinion, is still alive in the minds of older Japanese who will clench their teeth and bear suffering no matter how gruelling it is."

Group Orientation

In the past, I have written about how the education system in Japan forces students to coexist and persevere (Ganbare!*)* by purposely creating crowded, uncomfortable conditions. In classrooms of 30 – 45 students, in order to operate as a collective, everyone must discover his/her role and learn to work together in unison. Therefore, from childhood, the need for cooperation is drilled into the subconscious. One way to achieve this, which incidentally goes hand-in-hand with the densely populated classrooms, is the official decree that is heard numerous times throughout the school day: "*Junban!*" (順番). This literally translates to "order" but, more colloquially, means "Wait your turn." Writers such as Chris Weller have expressed awe and fascination with "Japan's love of line-forming," which he affirms "begins with the lessons kids learn as early as kindergarten." Linda Bennett, in her essay entitled *Expectations for Japanese Children*, points out how Japanese kids learn from all aspects of society: family, school, community, and even the nation, itself. "In each group (classroom)," she writes, "a child learns the self-discipline and commitment expected to be a supportive and responsible group member." As I continued to read the

Expectations, as laid-out by Ms. Bennett, I felt as though she was hinting at something which I discovered back in 2005: the Japanese psyche has been programmed more like that of a soldier than a normal civilian.

Army of the People

It is no secret that Article 9 of the Japanese Constitution (日本国憲法第 9 条) officially demilitarized the Armed Forces, leaving in its place a de facto peace-keeping squadron referred to as the Japan Self-Defense Forces. However, please never forget that, in Japan, situations are seldom what they appear to be on the surface. That is *tatemae*. On the other hand, if we examine the educational objectives of Japanese schools, and then compare them with the Seven Core Values (Loyalty, Duty, Respect, Selfless Service, Honor, Integrity, and Personal Courage) of the U.S. Army, we find that every Japanese citizen has been indoctrinated with a code of ethics which is startlingly similar to that of an American soldier. This is the deeper picture known as *honne*.

Loyalty, which means "bearing true faith and allegiance to the Constitution, the Army, your unit, and other soldiers" is equivalent to ***shakaisei*** (社会性), being socially conscious. For Japanese, the group is more important than the individual, and an individual should never stand out. Appropriate behavior includes being reserved, cooperative, and supportive of the group. Other relatable tenets expressed in the *Expectations* essay are: ***kyochosei*** (協調性), translated as "being cooperative or harmonious" and, ***yasashii*** (優しい), being kindhearted to members of the group.

Duty. This one is easy. Each person fulfilling their obligations ultimately impacts the greater society; therefore this tenet corresponds, first, to ***shakaisei*** and, on a more personal level, "studying hard" which is translated to ***susunde benkyo*** (進んで勉強). Please note that failure to perform one's duty results in shame—which can lead to a state which is similar to communal purgatory.

Respect along with **Loyalty** are principles which are constantly being imparted through the Confucian teachings that were adopted into the culture.

Selfless Service. Putting the welfare of the nation, the Army, and your fellow soldiers—i.e. the group—before your own is a foundational principle for every Japanese. ***Omoiyari*** (思いやり) is the ability to be sympathetic/empathetic to those around you.

Honor is ***meiyo*** (名誉) in Japanese. According to the U.S. Army, honor embodies the other six ethics: so it is a matter of carrying out the values of loyalty, duty, respect, selfless service, integrity and personal courage in everything you do. However, this is not honorable enough for Japanese; therefore, they came up with a more comprehensive code of honor containing eight virtues. You may have heard of it. It is called *Bushido*.

Integrity is a quality you develop by adhering to the moral principle of doing what's right for right's sake. This corresponds to ***hansei*** (反性), which is "self-discipline or self-reflection."

Personal Courage. The ability to live honorably on a consistent basis is the measuring stick; so ***jobu na*** (丈夫な), meaning "being strong and healthy," and ***gambaru*** (頑張る), "doing one's best and having persistence toward a goal" fit the bill nicely.

Ms. Bennett goes on to explain that each child is cared for by the whole society, and *all* Japanese adults are responsible for helping to teach the norms and customs of the society. For this reason, she claims, they are members of a "National Family." Once again, her description perfectly matches the relationship within the Armed Forces between officers (both commissioned as well as non-commissioned) and the lower-enlisted personnel. Oh, and let us not forget that, in school, most Japanese children wear uniforms and practice 'how to march' as well. Please think back to your school days. Do you recall having lessons on Drill and Ceremony?

Japanese Acceptance

Some foreigners complain about how Japanese are inflexible toward them. No matter how long they have lived in Japan, or how fluent they become in the language, or how accustomed they are to the culture, they are always treated as "outsiders." Let's take it a step further: over the years, I've had dozens of conversations and even received e-mails from disgruntled exchange students, foreign nationals, as well as teachers, who show little trepidation at using the "R-word," racism, to define the society's xenophobic attitude toward anything deemed not Japanese. Hearing first-hand accounts by the victims of biased mistreatment, most notably Brazilians, Koreans, and Peruvians, not to mention Ryukyuans, Ainu, and *Burakumin* (部落民), it would be difficult to argue otherwise. Nevertheless in regards to English-speaking Westerners, as we have discussed, the situation is different because when Japanese address the descendants of their conquerors their *Japanese Complex* triggers a passive response. So unless you are the type who compares inconveniences such as people on the train not wanting to sit next to you with life-threatening discriminatory acts like lynching, redlining, or false imprisonment—i.e. evidence of *real racism*—it might be necessary to come up with another term to describe the uncomfortable feeling commuters experience on their ride to and from work. Far beyond just being insulted on a personal level, bona-fide victims of real racism are attacked on institutional, cultural, structural, as well as interpersonal levels. The truth is, a large percentage of these "Japanese are racist" indictments have been lodged by *Japanophiles*. These people, usually from western nations, have fallen in love with their own perception of Japan and, in many cases, have become proficient in the language and perhaps a certain aspect of the culture. Their attitude and mannerisms, generally reflective of European values and standards, demand they be granted "white entitlement." Having been taught the western nations have conquered the countries inhabited by people of color, they believe it is only 'natural' for them to be liked and accepted. Therefore whenever these people bring up the topic of non-acceptance, I have to wonder if what they are really complaining about is how they are not being given preferential treatment.

For those who are not necessarily suffering from an elitist-complex, they may be failing to realize how their town or the company or school they work for functions like a military installation. In other words, being a foreigner in Japan has much in common with the status of a civilian on an Army post. If you have not gone through the requisite training, just buying something at the Post Exchange (PX), sporting camouflaged fatigues, or walking around the post does not make you a soldier. That said, just as it is possible for a civilian to undergo the necessary steps and take an oath to become a soldier, it is also possible to 'become Japanese.' In spite of what has been cited by contemporary, so-called experts on Japan to the contrary, there are numerous examples in the past and present of foreigners, especially from China and Korea, who have amalgamated into Japanese society. Having taken Japanese names makes it difficult to research their exact numbers but, the point is, foreigners being admitted into Japanese society is nothing new or impossible; it has been happening throughout history.

Before we put the idea of Japanese acceptance of foreigners entirely behind us, I just want to say that I do understand. I, too, wish Japanese were not so closed-minded in regards to their treatment of non-Japanese. And it would be nice to be stared at less and have people not feel intimidated to sit nearby during a daily commute. In short, non-Japanese want to be treated with the same compassion and respect that Japanese appear to provide toward their fellow countrymen. However in regards to 'being Japanese' this is less than half of the story. The irony is, if these *Japanophile* complainants actually understood how Japanese really behave when they are not being observed, in my opinion, most would completely discard the notion. By adhering to a Code which compels Japanese, especially women, to portray a cheerful demeanor or risk upsetting the apple cart, once away from public scrutiny it is only natural for them to experience some sort of relapse. When Westerners claim they rarely, if ever, witness Japanese raise their voice or disagree, this indicates the degree to which they are kept in the dark because, behind closed doors, supervisors harshly dressing down subordinates with rude, nasty remarks is the order of the day; and arguments are not uncommon either.

Only 1 Way

So let us fully unpack this idea of foreigners 'becoming Japanese.' Are you willing to adopt the idea of there being only one 'correct way' to approach any/every situation? Could you survive in an environment where there is no room for the individuality of doing your own thing? An easy example is *Seiza* (正座), which is translated as the "correct or proper way of sitting." Since Japanese are instructed there is only one correct way then, by default, all other forms of sitting are improper. Of course since the Meiji Era chairs have become commonplace in Japan but, despite this, in the mind of a Japanese person *seiza* is the only proper way to sit. Please be aware this type of thinking encompasses every life activity; so there is a proper or correct way to eat, walk, sleep, have your hair cut, so on and so forth. The Yamato Code even extends to simple traditions like sending and receiving postcards during the winter and summer holidays, or buying *omiyage* (お土産); these are souvenirs for coworkers, friends, and family members upon returning from a business trip or vacation. Depending on your personality these customs may evoke either sentiments of affection or, on the other hand, may seem quite trivial but, for Japanese, since they are mandatory, not optional, if asked their opinion they will probably be confused. For them, this question is similar to being asked about taxes or paying rent: no one likes to do it but the alternative—being homeless—is not really an option.

Mendokusai (面倒くさい), which is translated as "tedious, tiring, or troublesome", is the word that best describes how bothersome it is to constantly stay on-code by maintaining the harmony, known as *Wa* (和). For those who are determined to escape their blackness by immersing themselves into Japanese culture, here are some points to consider. How many of you are willing to adjust your behavior (the way you walk, when/what you eat, sleeping patterns, etc.) to be in accordance with the Japanese standard? An example of this is how men are expected to leave early in the morning, work all day, and return home late in the evening or at night. For women, the accepted working hours are somewhat lenient only because they are expected to be homemakers. I have met Japanese entrepreneurs who make money online or by some other unconventional means and, therefore, are not subject to any notion of a '9-5 workday.' Astonishingly some of these men feel pressure to leave their homes in the morning and stay out until evening; this to align themselves with the expected daily routine of a respectable husband. One man explained: "For Japanese it is disgraceful for a man to be at home all day." He claimed this would cast a negative light on the whole family. According to him: "If word got out I was sitting around the house all day—even if I make good money—it would damage my family's reputation so much I could never find suitable husbands to marry my daughters." Since 2021, the COVID-19 pandemic has forced many to work from home so, in the future, it will be interesting to see if this situation changes.

An office lady (OL) in her mid-forties, once asked me why I had chosen to live in Japan. Without hesitation, I ran-down the same song-and-dance-reply I always gave of wanting to connect with my Japanese roots and visit my ancestor's graves, etc. "*No,*" she cut me off in mid-sentence. "I mean, you used to be free…in America, right?" The urgency in her question threw me for a loop so I considered my next words carefully. "Are you saying in Japan people are not free?" Hearing this question grounded her to the present moment. "Never mind," she brushed me off, realizing she had went off-code. Nonetheless, in that momentary lapse, Kato-san had divulged more information than she could have imagined. Reflecting on the deeper meaning embedded in her question allowed me to expand my frame of thinking to where I was able to shrug-off extra stares on the train, recognizing I was probably unwittingly doing something which expresses freedom: i.e. doing something off-code. More times than not I found this to be the case. Usually it was something as innocent as humming or nodding my head to the music in my headphones—*both of which are serious glitches in the Japanese matrix!*

Understanding the Yamato Code has allowed me to preserve my identity and live peacefully in Japan. This, by the way, is no small feat in a country which assigns strict roles to limit expressions of free will. Although life is not perfect by any stretch of the imagination, whenever I am confronted in an unappealing way, by tapping into my knowledge of the Code, in most cases, not only do I avoid pitfalls but—and this is important—I am able to establish a precedent which discourages reoccurrences of this kind in the future. The ability to remain 'on your square' while saving face is a skill that few Japanese master, let alone someone not born-and-raised in the land of Yamato. Although it took over a decade of observation, surprisingly, my awareness of its existence began when I ceased to take personally any strange or peculiar happenings—especially anything seeming controversial. Having established my third-person perspective it became easy to see the Code for what it is: their religion, or even better, God's tenets. And accordingly, every year, thousands are sacrificed to the spirit of Yamato via suicide. Or, unable to endure the daily strain of having to conform, they become *hikikomori* (引きこもり) and bow-out of society altogether. Now let's discuss how to use the Code to save face.

Chapter 11: The Art of Saving Face

Although every society instructs their youth on acceptable behavior, many Westerners might be shocked by the considerable amount of time and effort invested by Japanese to understanding how to avoid any sort of social indiscretion which might result in public humiliation. This means learning how to save face. "It's been pounded into us so hard it has become instinct," explained Morimoto-sensei who, in addition to being a Buddhist priest, also taught History at a school where I worked. He claims this inclination has become so natural, so ingrained in every Japanese, he compared it to "a program which is constantly running in the background of our psyche." If you are wondering where this 'pounding into the psyche' is taking place, the answer is everywhere. But perhaps most importantly at school. If truth be told, at both public and private institutions, teaching students how to function in society—*not academic studies*—is the main curriculum. While students do have lessons in compulsory subjects like mathematics and science, a large portion of the education process occurs after school at *Gakushu Juku* (学習塾), or simply *Juku*. Morimoto-sensei explained that, in regards to cultivating both personal and professional relationships, the inability to save face is a 'deal breaker.' Unlike in western culture, where children are encouraged to assert themselves and think independently, Japanese are taught from pre-school to maintain the harmony and never rock the boat. Nevertheless since it is not possible to conduct oneself perfectly in every situation, behavior is constantly being policed in subtle ways by the greater society. Simply staring at whoever is deemed to be coloring outside the lines results in Japanese feeling a sense of shame. Please be aware any social indiscretion, mistake, or irregularity which is not supposed to happen (according to the script) is treated as a glitch in the matrix.

Administration of Shame

At the beginning of the 17th century, the Tokugawa Shogunate, obsessed with crushing any threat to its authority, encouraged Confucianism due to its focus on morality and ethics. One of the creeds which served this end came from a 12th century Confucian scholar, *Chu Hsi* (朱熹), due to his belief in unwavering loyalty and duty to one's parents...*and rulers*. Today, aspects of this teaching are still evident in the steadfast devotion Japanese have for their school, company, or just society in general. Jonathon Rice, author of *Behind the Japanese Mask*, calls Confucianism "the moral underpinning of the Japanese way of life." Nonetheless the question one must ask is: How is this unfailing dedication to the values of society so thoroughly programmed into each and every person? According to Master Kǒng himself, otherwise known as Confucius (孔夫子), the solution lies in creating an atmosphere where the slightest deviance from normalcy leads to a personal sense of shame:

"If you control people by punishment, they will avoid crime, but have no personal sense of shame. If you govern by means of virtue and control them with propriety, they will gain their own sense of shame and thus correct themselves."

~The Analects

Wa (和) implies peaceful relations among members of a
social group but, in reality, it is far from tranquil. Considered
integral to Japanese society, individuals who dare to go
against the grain are reprimanded by a tidal wave of
disapproval by superiors, family members, and colleagues via
methods which might be hard for Westerners to imagine. This
is simply because, in many cases, words are never exchanged.
"The nail that sticks out gets hammered down" (出る釘は打
たれる) is the famous adage which best expresses the
immense societal pressure placed on Japanese to conform. In
such a homogenous-thinking society, unless you're a
politician or an entertainer, standing out from the crowd is not
only frowned upon, it results in being marginalized to a state
of *communal purgatory*. Ian Buruma, who is the author of a
number of books on Japan, states: "Social rules, rather than
an abstract system of morals, control Japanese behaviour." It
took several years of working in Japanese schools, both
public and private, before I realized the priority of the faculty
was not formal education but, rather, to teach the children to
be Japanese: i.e. show them their place within the societal
framework. Having an average of 38 students in each
homeroom, since students do not change classes for each
subject, with the exception of Phys Ed and labs, they are
forced to stay-put in the same, overcrowded classroom for 8 -
10 hours. In most cases, this even includes lunch. It is here,
through constant trial, trauma, and tribulation, where the
collective subconscious is programmed with the idea that
'we' in this classroom must struggle together (*Ganbare!*).
Along with this is the unspoken truth that accompanies such
reasoning: all those outside 'our world' are insignificant.
Concurrent with the nurturing of this 'Us only' mentality is
the Confucian teaching to respect authority. Young people

learn their role, for the time being, is to sit down, be quiet, and follow directions—which brings us back to the edict of teachers 'showing them their place.' Put another way, while there are lessons on math, science, and history being taught, the goal of the Ministry of Education, Culture, Sports, Science and Technology (文部科学省), also known as M.E.X.T., is not to raise test scores or elevate students' intellect so much as it is to put every youth on-code. The Yamato Code. This is the true religion. And just like Marine boot-camp or any training program designed to get people on the 'same page,' not only is it necessary to eradicate critical-thinking but, in addition, to cancel any notion of independence or existing apart from the group. With so much academic study occurring at evening *juku* lessons, this allows schools to operate along strict guidelines which bear a closer resemblance to military training than formal education.

Social Totalitarianism: To be or not to be Japanese

Totalitarianism is a political system that prohibits any opposition whatsoever to the government. Regarded as a form of authoritarianism, it exercises an extremely high degree of control over public and private affairs. Mao Zedong, former Chairman of the Communist Party in China, Joseph Stalin, former leader of the Soviet Union, along with Adolf Hitler, led prototypical totalitarian regimes. In contrast to these dictatorships, the programming and the pressure to 'be Japanese' is not coming from the government per se but, instead, is being imposed on the people—*by the people themselves*. Each Japanese heart yearns to beat in accordance with the drumbeat of society: this is the Yamato spirit. For this reason, instead of Shinto, Buddhism, or Confucianism, perhaps it would be more appropriate to call the Japanese religion something with 'Yamato' in it. Or we can simply call it *tatemae* which, after all, is the embodiment of social totalitarianism because anyone who does not comply with the Japanese programming is subject to punishment by the societal thought-police who regulate through a special type of bullying called *Ijime* (イジメ, 虐め). A former colleague of mine, Watanabe-sensei, explained that "*ijime* is as much a part of Japanese culture as *sushi*, sumo wrestling, or green tea." So accordingly, when Shinnosuke Komatsuda, a 15-year-old boy from Saitama Prefecture, committed suicide in September 2019 due to being the target of bullying at school, even though it was no secret as to what took place, no one was surprised to hear the boy's mother blame the school and ask for a full investigation. *Why?* Because she was reading from 'the script.' This is what grieving parents of bullied victims always say on the news. In other words, what else could she do? Admit she had failed to teach her son the values of society? She, along with everyone else, knows her son either could not, or would not, adjust to the standard that had been set by the homeroom—his society—and therefore he was sacrificed. At that point, her only concern was to be granted a reprieve. Not only was she grieving the death of her son, she was being singled-out, which we've already defined as communal purgatory; so in order to 'save face' she had to say what was expected of her. The essay entitled *Shame, Honor, and Duty* really drives this point home:

*"Why does shame have to be avoided at all costs? In Japan, relationships between people are greatly affected by duty and obligation. In duty-based relationships, what **other** people believe or think has a more powerful impact on behavior than*

what the individual believes. Shame occurs through others'
negative feelings towards you or through your feelings of
having failed to live up to your obligations...but in Japanese
culture, shame cannot be removed until a person does what
society expects."

~Dr. Takako McCrann, Ph.D.

"Shit Rolls Downhill"

To fully illustrate the tedious subtleties of feeling shame with
respect to saving face, allow me to share another trying
experience. Back in 2000, I was a basketball coach and
English teacher at a small high school in Hamamatsu City,
which is in Shizuoka Prefecture. It is also important to note
that I was employed through the J.E.T. Programme. The
Japanese Exchange and Teaching Program is probably the
largest and most well-known organization in Japan associated
with ESL education. Every year, hundreds of native-English
speakers are brought to Japan to serve as
teachers/ambassadors of their homeland. It is a great program
for anyone who is interested in a short stint of experiencing
life over here. At one point, during my 3-year stay at Jonan
High School, payday fell on a holiday-weekend. According to
my contract, in such an event, we were supposed to be paid
on the Friday prior to the weekend but, for some reason, I was
not. Initially, upon realizing this, I was not upset because I
did not have any special plans for the weekend. However I
decided it was prudent to report the incident to the clerk who
was in-charge of finances. So, that afternoon just after lunch,
I went to the main-office of my school. Clerks in schools and
companies are oftentimes overworked and, for this reason, I
just assumed it was an oversight.

But I was wrong.

After I explained the situation to one of the clerks in the office, he immediately went to the rear of the room and reported to an older man sitting at a desk. This man was the office-supervisor. After a few seconds of listening to the younger man, the old man did not even try to hide his contempt. Because he was at the rear of the room and there were five other clerks between us, some speaking to coworkers or on the phone, plus the fact he tended to use a colloquial dialect, I did not understand everything he said. However the sudden scowl which formed on his face could not be mistaken, especially when it was followed by the pejorative "gaijin." He eventually pointed at a woman who was sitting at her desk; she was still finishing the last remnants of her *bento*. "Ikeda!" he rudely yelled across the room, failing to use the honorific "-*san*" after her name which is how workers, even supervisors, usually address each other. There are exceptions to this rule, such as employees whose relationship has become somewhat friendly but, in this case, the suffix usually becomes -*kun* or -*chan*. Simply put, for him to shout "Ikeda!" in front of everyone while she was eating was definitely impolite. Having myself been raised in a verbally abusive home, my heart instantly went out to Ms. Ikeda. That is until I realized her coping mechanism to deal with this type of frustration was to pass it onto someone she deemed lower on the totem-pole than herself. In this case it was someone who she mistook for a helpless gaijin.

I have already discussed how Japanese society functions similar to the chain of command in the military. While in the Army I frequently heard the phrase: "Shit rolls downhill!" This means, as a rule, the consequences of any lousy decisions or negative actions by the commanders 'roll downhill' to the lower-ranking subordinates.

I watched Ms. Ikeda take a few last bites before proceeding to stuff the napkins, chopsticks, and other remains into her lunchbox. From my vantage point, this seemed a bit strange considering lunchtime had been over for nearly half an hour. Minutes later she finally sauntered up to the window where I had been patiently waiting. Ikeda-san was a typical looking clerk. Very slim, she was dressed in a white collared blouse and a loose-fitting, gray skirt which almost touched her bony knees. Her stringy hair, which was perm-free and lacked any style, hung limply above her shoulders. As she approached I noticed her large, oval glasses made her eyeballs appear much bigger than they actually were. While I explained the situation for a second time, just like her *sempai*, Ms. Ikeda went out of her way to be insulting—*the woman was still chewing food!* When I finished speaking she took a moment to lazily swallow like she was bored before uttering: "You'll be paid next week."

End of discussion.

As she walked away, I noticed everyone in the office was now silent. One clerk was looking in my direction while the remainder pretended to concentrate on their computer screens. Nonetheless it was obvious everyone was listening to our conversation. In contrast, if a similar situation occurred in the United States in which an office worker made a mistake that could easily be proven by a glance at a contract—and her response to my inquiry was to then double-down on her error with open disrespect—I would have verbally slayed her on the spot. In such a case, by western standards, the contract is the code. However, in Japan, nothing is above the Yamato Code—not even a legally binding contract. At this point I knew it was imperative to maintain my dignity. "*Sumimasen,*" I called out to Ikeda-san's receding silhouette. Before I could say anything else her boss came to the rescue. "*Mou owari!*" he shouted in defiance, indicating I should just shut-up and leave. Following his raucous macho-man display, when he saw me still waiting at the window (which, by the way, was borderline off-code), he exhaled in disgust before rising from his desk to confront me.

Although becoming visibly upset is normally taboo, considering his rank in the chain-of-command, his rebuke equated to a senior-official putting a subordinate in his place: i.e. he was hammering down an unruly, wayward nail. By the time the office-supervisor approached the window he was so smug and sure of his superior position, he never considered his own words could be used against him. After looking me up and down, he called me a fool who didn't know what he was talking about. "Nowhere in the contract does it say you're to be paid on any Friday—holiday or no holiday!" As he shouted I was glad he was on the other side of the window because there were small bits of food and spit flying from his mouth. In spite of this distraction, I did not miss how he was misconstruing the facts. "You have two versions," he said, "one typed in Japanese and the other in English, right?"

"*Hai*", I coolly responded in an unemotional tone. This belied how much I really wanted to smack him across the face.

"Well," he continued, "the Japanese contract isn't the same as the English one." He then explained how he's "not concerned" with what he called the "gaijin contract" before concluding his perverse litany with a personal jibe. He complained that gaijin should learn how to read Japanese.

"*Sou-desuka*," I calmly replied. While not questioning his authority, I was not quite agreeing either. "*Wakarimashita.*" After assuring him I understood, I slightly nodded and walked away. As I did so my mind was reeling. *Did he really believe I was stupid enough to buy into his rhetoric about the contracts being different?*

There are two points worth mentioning. First, considering the date to be paid was clearly printed in the contract, had I lashed out on that afternoon and made a scene, once the smoke cleared, the supervisor would have been forced to concede. However, overshadowing any contract discrepancy, the fact I displayed total disregard for the chain of command by telling-off a supervisor, this disturbance of the harmony would have almost certainly supplanted the supervisor's unethical actions as the point of focus. This means, in the eyes of the staff, I would have been the 'bad guy.' Following this line of thinking, I would not have gotten paid any faster and the supervisor probably would have received nothing more than a slap on the wrist. Nevertheless the real consequence would have been felt in the forthcoming days, weeks and months by the 'cold-shoulder' treatment I received from coworkers. The fact is, in all likelihood, I probably would have been coerced into quitting—just like my predecessor—which leads into the second point. The native-English teacher from the previous year had suddenly quit during the spring-semester. According to circulating rumors, he had been the target of abuse by both staff and students. It was for this reason, the principal later divulged at the end-of-year party, he had selected me as the replacement. Having spent the past six years as a social-worker in the United States, this convinced him that I was a good fit for the job. Over heated flasks of Japanese *sake* called *atsukan*, the principal stated that, upon initially arriving at Jonan High School (a few months before me), he was appalled to find there was no native-English teacher. After ascertaining the facts of the matter, he became determined to find "an individual who was psychologically stable and understood Japanese thinking." In hindsight, I certainly had no idea of the existence of any code. Nevertheless considering throughout the entire ordeal my attitude and actions were on-code to a tee, perhaps it can be said my Yamato ancestors guided me...*now back to the story.*

Since it was an extended weekend, this gave me enough time to have some well-educated Japanese read the contract. All three confirmed what I already knew: the office-supervisor at my school—amongst other things—was a liar. On the evening before returning to work, I called the assistant director of the J.E.T. Programme in our prefecture. He resided in Shizuoka City, which is the capital. Marc was a friendly Euro-American guy who, like me, was a former paratrooper from Fort Bragg. For this reason, I had his cell phone number. Once he verified I should have already been paid (after all he had been), he promised to report the incident. At the time, I did not think this would be necessary because my ego had been assuaged; but I refrained from saying anything due to the reputation of his supervisor, Suzuki-san: she was known for not taking any bullshit. Nicknamed the "Iron Butterfly," this lady represented much of the aspirations of modern Japanese women. Highly educated and familiar with western culture, what distinguished her from the average Eigo-hoe was she had not sacrificed *Yamato-nadeshiko* (大和撫子) which, for Japanese, describes idealized ladylike etiquette. Confident and assertive but not in the manner of a western woman, if not stunning, Ms. Suzuki was definitely elegant—hence the illustrious pseudonym.

The next morning at 7:55 am, I received a call from Marc while I was cycling to school. Due to a special ceremony that morning he was already at work. After the greeting, he surprised me by handing the phone to Ms. Suzuki. She told me, in no uncertain terms, if the office-staff did not admit their mistake and make amends to *my* satisfaction that she, herself, would pay a personal visit to Jonan High School. *Wow!* I thought, more than a little impressed at the support I was receiving from the Iron Butterfly. Now it is important to note that while I did feel slighted by the office-supervisor, in my mind, as long as I got paid, I was not planning on making any more waves. The truth is, I hoped the incident was over but, of course, this was not the case.

"*Ohayo,*" I responded to students who greeted me at the school entrance. As I walked through the hallway and climbed the stairs to the second-floor, I felt as relaxed as could be expected considering I was arriving to work. However everything changed as soon as I entered the teacher's room. Walking through the door, not only did every single faculty member flatly ignore my attempts to greet them, not one dared to even make eye-contact. I felt invisible. Initially I told myself it was my imagination; that is, until I arrived at my desk and noticed *every* teacher who sat in my row was curiously away from their desk. This reminded me of the scenario that kids in Jersey and NYC described as 'being hot.' This situation could arise for a number of reasons, the most common being if a person was wanted by police, suspected of being a snitch, or had 'beef' with someone of notoriety. In such cases, bystanders weren't taking any chances of being arrested as an accomplice, getting attacked or, even worse, catching a stray bullet. "*I got more glocks and techs than you/ I make it hot / niggas won't even stand next to you…*" This is how *Biggie* and *Method Man* expressed it. In short, everyone makes sure to stand clear.

"*Minna-san, ohayo-gozaimasu!*" Once the *chorei* (朝礼) commenced, which is the morning meeting, I was jolted from my thoughts back to reality. Following ten minutes of listening to the vice principal's announcements, I watched him quickly scurry out of the room. As I was considering what the emergency might be, it was then I felt a level of relief because someone finally acknowledged me. "*Amaru-sensei, ohayo-gozaimasu.*" It was the voice of Yamamoto-sensei, who was the young lady who sat next to me but, for some reason, had decided to listen to the announcements while standing on the far-side of the room. Swiveling in my chair to return her cheerful greeting my smile quickly faded when I noticed that in addition to Ms. Yamamoto another English teacher who did not particularly like me, Ishikawa-sensei, along with our supervisor, a man named Otake-sensei, were standing behind her. "We have a scheduled-meeting downstairs," Ms. Yamamoto explained. Now I understood the reason for the vice principal's sudden departure.

As the four of us left the teachers room, the faculty members in the hallway gave us a wide berth. But now they were openly staring. Everyone except me seemed to know what was going on. This feeling, in addition to how no one else from our department was joining us, was a 'red-flag' this was not just some ordinary meeting. As we descended the staircase, I glanced at the back of Otake-sensei's head, who was leading the way. In Japan, maintaining the hierarchy is an indispensable part of staying on code. Therefore right behind our supervisor was Ishikawa-san, who was second in seniority, and bringing up the rear was Yamamoto-san and myself. Although I tried to elicit details from Ms. Yamamoto about what was happening she feigned ignorance, claiming she was not sure either. Upon arriving to the main office, one of the clerks promptly ushered us past the desks and into the principal's office, which was a smaller room adjoining the main office. As we entered, I was expecting to see the short, stocky silhouette of the principal but he was not there. Instead, sitting at the desk was the vice principal with his tall, lanky frame, white hair, and silver spectacles. And standing next to him was the main-office supervisor. The two men were facing us and both had grim expressions on their faces. The atmosphere had the look and feel of a disciplinary hearing.

"Thank you all for coming." Following a formal salutation by the vice principal he wasted no time before gesturing to the man to his left. "Matsumoto-san has requested this meeting." As soon as he was handed the floor, Mr. Matsumoto immediately walked over to me and stuck his finger in my face like a drill-sergeant. Then he started shouting. Considering how many times I had been the recipient of such tongue-lashings in the Army, especially in basic training, it was not difficult to maintain my cool. The worst part was being in such close proximity to Matsumoto-san. The fact he was much shorter helped but it was still not easy to look at his pockmarked face and brown teeth—not to mention his breath smelled awful!

Listening to him, I was taken aback he was sticking to his story about discrepancies in the contracts even though he knew Otake-san, as well as the ladies, could read both copies. For subordinates, whenever a senior official is speaking, a major part of staying on code is to either agree or simply remain silent. Having finished talking about the contract, he then recounted my visit last Friday to the main office. In doing so he called me 'rude,' 'stupid,' used the word 'gaijin' twice and, most grievous of all, falsely accused me of insubordination. At this point, I was starting to lose patience. When he directed his attention to my supervisor, Otake-sensei, claiming it was his fault for not training me properly, I surreptitiously took a half-step backwards…*but his breath was still booming!*

Since formal proceedings in Japan remind me of the military, I relied on what I had learned in the Army and never attempted to speak until the vice principal gave me permission. Once he did, I began in Japanese but soon realized it was more advantageous to speak English. Understanding the ladies were there to translate, I also figured the time it took to convert English to Japanese gave me precious seconds to think. Minutes later, when Matsumoto-san tried to interrupt Ms. Ishikawa while she was still interpreting my words, I decided to go on offense. So I interrupted him right back—but with an apology. "Sir," I said looking right at him, "I really am sorry to have inconvenienced not only you but everyone here…please understand this was not my intention." While this was translated I turned my head toward the vice principal. "Mr. Matsumoto is claiming the Japanese contract and the English contract are not the same. Well, over the weekend, I reported this matter to Suzuki-san, who is also one of my supervisors…" At the mere mention of the 'Iron-Butterfly' a silent hush filled the room. "For some reason," I continued, "she doesn't seem to think there is any discrepancy between the Japanese and English versions of the contract." After Yamamoto-san translated this, I switched back to Japanese. "Oh, and by the way, Suzuki-san said that if I am not satisfied with how Mr. Matsumoto handles this incident she will be paying a personal visit to Jonan High School."

In Japanese, English, or any language, there are no words to describe the sudden 180-degree 'about-face' which occurred at this precise moment. It was no less striking than if you were fast asleep in a tranquil, pitch-dark room and, suddenly, music started blaring as the curtains were opened, exposing the room to bright sunlight: the entire atmosphere was now different. From this point, three things occurred which I found very astonishing. What impressed me most was how everyone in the room—without a single word being spoken—comprehended the office-supervisor had been trumped. This included Mr. Matsumoto himself. After a split-second lull, the next words spoken came from the vice principal. And when I say he lashed-out at Mr. Matsumoto that is exactly what happened—yelling, screaming, and cursing him out. He then told Matsumoto-san to open the door and call Ms. Ikeda, who was in the adjacent office, no doubt listening to every word of our meeting. Having been summoned by her superiors, when Ms. Ikeda appeared, I noticed her demeanor was somewhat contrary to the other day. Gone was the laid-back posture…*and she definitely was not chewing any food!*

"*Hai,*" she uttered in a frightful tone after running inside the room. Once the vice principal finished giving both of them a further tongue-lashing he ordered them to apologize—and I mean the deepest form of apology which is called *Dogeza* (土下座). After the teachers moved to the side, the two clerks walked over and prostrated themselves on their knees before me. Placing both hands together on the floor, with their backs straight, they then lowered their heads down onto their hands, thereby kowtowing like I was the *daimyo*, Oda Nobunaga. "Amaru-sensei," began Matsumoto-san in earnest. Being the *sempai*, it was his responsibility to assume the role of spokesperson. "We are sincerely sorry. We have no excuse for our unruly actions!"

Quite shocked at this sudden turn of events and somewhat embarrassed, I simply replied "*Hai,*" and left it at that.

After regaining their feet, Mr. Matsumoto whispered something to Ikeda-san and she promptly left the room. Because he had spoken under his breath, the only phrase I understood was "Hurry up!" It was then the second most astonishing event occurred. Mr. Matsumoto stepped closer and with a brown-toothed grin offered to lend me money until my paycheck had been processed. Now I, along with everyone else, understood what Ikeda-san had been ordered to 'hurry up' and do. This prompted another verbal dress-down by the vice principal. By the time the meeting adjourned, I was glad to finally leave the office and have things return to normal. Nevertheless, due to the third astonishing event, this never happened. As the four of us walked back to the teacher's room, there was a noticeable difference in the order of our formation. I was now leading the group alongside Otake-sensei. Feeling a bit uneasy, not once but twice, I tried to slow down to speak with Ms. Yamamoto, who was walking behind us with Ms. Ishikawa. To my dismay, whenever I did this, the entire group followed suit and stopped. This is when it dawned on me that, like it or not, anyone who saves face in a disciplinary hearing with the vice principal and the main-office supervisor gets a promotion.

The next morning, when I arrived to the teacher's room, not only did I receive more than my share of greetings from the faculty, Ikeda-san was there waiting at my desk. On the previous evening, I later found out, when the principal returned from his business trip and received reports about what had taken place, both she and Mr. Matsumoto received another reading of the riot act and, furthermore, Ikeda-san was ordered to apologize the following morning in front of the entire faculty. This time however, to my relief, she did not kneel on the floor. Later that day I was summoned to the main office so she could apologize again, this time in front of the clerks. So, in all, Ms. Ikeda had to publicly apologize three times for a lousy decision made by her supervisor. This illustrates how in Japan, like the military, *shit rolls downhill!*

In Summary

What tipped the scale in my favor was I did not overreact to pressure from coworkers or any of Mr. Matsumoto's antics, which included insults and other such provocation. Confident I had 'right' on my side afforded me the patience to wait for an opportunity and, once presented, I merely stated the facts and never lost my composure. The cameo appearance by the Iron Butterfly was just the icing on the cake. Following this simple guideline allowed the Yamato Code to perform its function: which is to expose those who are in violation of its edicts and, subsequently, to hammer them into place. Any overreaction on my part would have removed the Japanese official who was violating principles such as *meiyo* (honor) and *hansei* (integrity) from the spotlight, and I would have been stigmatized as a typical example of an angry or unruly gaijin. Not only does this incident demonstrate how regardless of a person's status or position the consensus of the group dominates but, more importantly, it confirms that anyone who is recognized by the group as reflecting the precepts of the Code—even a so-called *hafu* or foreigner—cannot, at the same time, be disrespected or treated as a gaijin. Owing to this circumstance the space to build my square was realized.

In part 1, we discussed how people have been programmed to process ideas as dichotomous constructs. Since the Japanese universe consists of only Japanese or non-Japanese, it is obvious in which polarity gaijin exist; but in the midst of this scheme are foreign-nationals who refuse to reside with orthodox gaijin on the wrong side of the tracks. What these individuals have in common is an understanding (perhaps unconsciously) of how, in this society, Japanese vs. gaijin is nothing more than contrasting humans and sub-humans. This, being the real duality, is the awareness which invariably leads a person into the eye of the storms. As previously stated, this book is written in black and white—not shades of gray.

A Peek at Life in Nippon...

Top: Taking a sip at a shrine

Bottom: English Camp (2000)

89

Top Left: Mayor Kitawaki with AfroA

Top Right: AfroAsiatic debut CD (2000)

Bottom Left: At a sound check

Bottom: Right: Chillin' with James "Source" Elmore

Top: Assistant coach of 2001 Shizuoka Champions

Bottom: As a player in Kakegawa, I was unstoppable!

Osaka & Tokyo

Top left: The famous Dotonbori

Top Right: *Shotengai* (shopping district) in Osaka

Middle right: Nightlife in Osaka

Bottom left: *Shotengai* in Shibuya, Tokyo

The Real Talk Community

Top: School opening (2018)

Middle: Community Forum

Bottom: Hanging out with Sterlyn

Real Talk Halloween Party

Top 3 pics: Adults and children having fun at "Jambu Island" (food truck name).

Bottom: Patrick Bradley & I choppin' it up.

Part 4: Observations & Strategy

The first three sections contain information necessary for creating a lane to establish your square, including the paramount importance of calibrating one's actions and behavior to maintain face; so all that remains is to take what we have learned and convert it to useful knowledge. While it is undeniable the Yamato Code is the source of angst and overwhelming pressure on its citizens, on the other hand, it's also their all-powerful, energy reservoir symbolizing Japanese solidarity as well as prosperity. Please go back and study this ethical blueprint with the understanding it regulates Japanese attitudes and behavior. Once you understand the rules of the game, the challenge is to master its precepts to where they can be spun in such a way to serve your needs. The ability to navigate the society with a minimum of stress gives a person a shot at a life worth living; but this can only occur with both feet firmly planted. Let us begin with some observations you must never forget or dismiss.

Chapter 12: Alienation

Although the measures taken may not be as obvious as those favored by J-Spex, *always* expect to be subjected to some degree of *otherization*. There are few exceptions. Even for Japanese who are not interested in English and, by and large, have no problem with speaking their language to non-Japanese, they usually feel obligated to use English in their opening or closing remarks. Why is there such an urgency to say '*Haro?*' Or finish a conversation with "*See you*" or "*Sank yoo* (Thank you)?" This also includes back-handed compliments like "Your Japanese is so good" or praising your ability to use chopsticks. While on the surface (*tatemae*) these seem to be nothing more than polite gestures, by now, it should be understood Japanese do this as a reminder that *you* are a foreigner (*honne*). Another embedded subtlety is the confirmation to any Japanese in the vicinity that she/he is on code. So no matter what, never forget—because Japanese cannot—their universe consists of only two types of people: Japanese and foreigners. The only other possibility is the biracial designation *Hafu* which, at best, is a superficial term. In recent years, with the rise of athletes like Naomi Osaka and Rui Hachimura, the *hafu* label has gained so much popularity in the media that some youngsters insist it (or gaijin) is cool. This is no different from how adolescent white kids are known to go through a 'black phase' in which they emulate their favorite rapper, athlete, or cool dude in the neighborhood but, by their mid-twenties, have long since discarded the trendy fashion, cornrows, or dreadlocks to assume their position within the dominant society.

The idea of foreigners 'becoming Japanese' has been mentioned and how, throughout history, this is nothing new. But, again, who in their right-mind really wants to renounce their own culture and values and, without reservation, subject themselves to a rigid system designed to control their every thought and action? While it is true the goal is to discard the 'gaijin designation,' this is not being done in order to join anything, or become anyone, other than who you are: a human being. To tread these waters, a person must be determined to stand on principle and high values. More importantly, he/she cannot be afraid to defend them. Truthfully, this is one of the biggest determining factors as to whether or not a foreigner is a gaijin. Even *Japanophiles* who complain about being *otherized*, at the end of the day, recognize they are gaijin but, for some reason, have become obsessed with acquiring skin-deep accoutrements of acceptance. Not unlike the 1960s civil-rights activists in the United States that suffered so many indecencies at the hands of whites who refused to integrate their lunch counters, *Japanophiles* want to pretend they are members of the greater society. Looking at news footage of that Woolworth in Greensboro, North Carolina, I still wonder why those blacks were so determined to have a cup of coffee next to people who obviously hated them.

In this regard, *21st Century Japan Decoded* does not promote forcing oneself onto Japanese society like some needy orphan. Instead, stand your ground and assert the right to be your natural self. Something worth mentioning is that even after drawing a line in the sand and establishing your square, Japanese will usually test your resolve once or twice a year. This usually occurs in January or April, both of which are cyclical starting points on their calendar; so you may be required to renew your 'Gaikokujin membership' on an annual basis, so to speak. Concerning this stance there is one possible downside. Standing on your square automatically provides an independence not afforded to run-of-the-mill gaijin. However, depending on your personality, this can be interpreted as either a 'breath of fresh air' or a lonely place to be. During the growth stages of any successful person there are, inevitably, periods of solitude. A person with her inner-resources intact uses these moments of detachment for inward reflection.

Since Japan, unlike most countries, does not single-out blacks from other foreigners, this unique situation should cause these fragmented people to realize something they have forgotten but everyone else has not: it is mutually beneficial to support one another. All throughout history people have formed alliances to achieve shared goals or defeat a common enemy. Considering the majority of blacks in Japan have so much in common, for instance, they are usually gainfully employed college graduates from middle-class backgrounds who are confronted by the same challenges of (1) being victimized by the global system of racism/white supremacy and (2) being alienated by Japanese society, at some point, it seems only natural the western programming of their subconscious which engenders contempt and distrust for other blacks, what I call *Tribal Programming*, might phase itself out.

Whether blacks in Japan forever remain gaijin is not my concern. That said, I will admit what is to become of these melanin-rich residents more than holds my interest. What is the future-legacy of black people on this island-nation? In thirty years, will anything have changed? By then, do you think blacks will still resemble the educated but otherwise mediocre lot we see now? A non-collective of individuals who, by and large, exist separately doing their own thing? While some are making strides in fields like business, education, or entertainment, how many of these ambitious go-getters are hiring other blacks? Or moving their families to Japan? Will any of this change by 2051? Who knows? My objective is to assist those who wish to elevate themselves. After that let the chips fall where they may.

For anyone who grows up with a parent in the military, moving from place to place as well as changing schools is unavoidable. As a child trying to make friends, my father told me, "Never beg for anyone's acceptance." Instead he emphasized I should illustrate, through my words and actions, that I was someone worthy of friendship. Likewise blacks should never attempt to persuade Japanese (or anyone) to accept them. Within the circle of coworkers and acquaintances, once your actions consistently reflect their code of conduct, they are all but required to discard much of the gaijin treatment or risk losing face themselves. Using this to your advantage is key to creating space. The goal is to find the 'eye' between the storms. Believe it or not, it begins with something as simple as your own self-identification. For instance your own name. Do you think demanding to be addressed in a certain way is petty? We live in an age wherein transgender women—even those with clear traces of a beard and mustache—can claim legal compensation in a court of law for being called 'sir.' What does this say about the value today's society places on addressing people?

At high schools, universities, and language-conversation centers called *Eikaiwas* (英会話), a common question I get from Westerners is: "Why do Japanese call you by your last name?" Some even phrase it as: "How did you get them to call you Amaru-sensei instead of by your first name?" Moreover they are usually curious as to why Japanese, in particular staff members and coworkers, communicate with me in their language instead of English. It is easy to assume the reason is my language ability. While this is partially true, considering my proficiency is far from fluent, I assure you this is not the only explanation. Unbeknownst to them, these inquiries can be merged into one question: *How are you able to circumvent the Yamato Code?* Until about ten years ago, I used to respond to this quite frankly. However I stopped doing so because, simply put, nobody believed my answer.

For Japanese in professional relationships with Westerners there are systematic rules of conduct. Perhaps at the top of the list is speaking English. And be forewarned, this pertains even to people from France, Germany, Italy, or other non-English-speaking countries because Japanese believe *all* foreigners speak English. Another tenet is to address non-Japanese by their first names plus the honorific –san or –*sensei* (and in many cases, they will drop the honorific suffix altogether) while Japanese address each other by their *last names* attached with the appropriate honorific. This corresponds to the western custom of using Mr. / Ms. or Professor before the family name. Hmm, let's think for a moment: if students in the United States or Canada, as a rule, insisted on calling their foreign-language teachers by their first names, would this not be considered disrespectful? Or discriminatory? As a high school student, instead of addressing your Spanish teacher as Mr. Gonzalez, can you imagine calling him 'Mr. Pedro' or, even worse, just 'Pedro?'

Recognizing Teaching Moments

Learning to associate annoying situations with teaching opportunities took a number of years. In all honesty, back in the day, they used to piss me off. Let's not forget that I, too, am Japanese; so I feel a special responsibility to teach *my* people correctly. Having come to the understanding that Japanese, upon first meeting non-Japanese, feel obligated to ask redundant questions, I concentrated on learning how to side-step these Gaijin Interviews and, by doing so, to avoid the frustration I always felt following these mindless interrogations. The best and easiest way to escape most types of unwanted dialogue is to assert yourself as the *sempai*; in this instance this means the person who is leading the conversation. Once it has been established who is asking the questions, if a newly-made acquaintance is still intent on an interview, I usually comply. However I turn it around by asking them to introduce themselves; so the would-be interviewer ends up divulging his life story. Assigning Japanese the subordinate position either puts them off or, in a best-case-scenario, you could end up meeting a cool person who really does want to interact with you and, for this reason, is eager to answer your questions—this, as opposed to the person who only has an interest in being entertained by a random foreigner. As mentioned, this technique is remarkably efficient but, as time went by, I realized many Japanese found it so hard to rebound after losing-face they became uncomfortable in my presence and, in fact, some would make an effort to avoid interactions with me altogether. Understanding this method has the potential to crush egos, I have become somewhat cautious in its implementation because it is not my intention to 'throw the baby out with the bathwater' by slamming the door on an otherwise decent person who, by international standards, might be a bit socially awkward. However the foremost reason I sometimes allow myself to be questioned is I noticed these interviews provide an opportunity to 'blow their minds' by saying something they have never heard.

Whether you allow yourself to be interviewed or not is strictly a personal decision. However if you are approached by a total stranger, you should NEVER answer any of their questions until the solicitor has (1) identified him/herself, (2) explained what their relationship is to you and (3) clearly defined their purpose for approaching you. Please remember that if you do not comply with being interviewed, the person may lose face because asking questions to strangers is taboo behavior according to the Yamato Code.

There is one common theme in my interviews: they rarely follow the established (J-Spex) protocol. Before I reply to any of their questions, I normally have them give a short self-intro. After all, they want to meet me, right? In regards to my personal bio, after carefully listening to the Japanese person's self-introduction, I try to stick to the same topics he/she talked about. That said, in most cases, I refrain from divulging details about my age, marital status, or place of birth unless I feel the information is relevant. Eventually, the conversation usually focuses on "America," which I've found really means white people or western society. But some Japanese ask specific questions about black people. Whenever I'm faced with broad questions about Americans, I insist they clarify to whom they are referring. "Do you mean Black people? White people? Hindus? Jews? The rich? The middle class? Those living in the city? The countryside?" If they appear confused, I take this opportunity to implement a teaching moment by explaining how much of the developed world is not homogeneous like Japan where everyone follows the same culture. Therefore, in the United States, whatever Whites are doing or thinking may or may not include Blacks, Latinos, Arabs, or Asians. To emphasize the point, I like to put the shoe on the other foot by asking them about what's going on in Seoul or Beijing before explaining that, identical to how Japanese see foreigners as one group, many Americans see Asians similarly. For questions about black people, since these inquiries demonstrate a more profound curiosity, I do not hesitate to dive deeper down the rabbit-hole by explaining how blacks in the United States represent an array of religions, culture, and values. Depending on my audience, I might even explain distinctions that exist among blacks such as the difference between militants, religious zealots, street entrepreneurs, and even *coons*. This conversation never fails to surprise them.

To be clear, I am not necessarily promoting Gaijin Interviews as a way to raise conscious-awareness. This is just what I do. In short, you should convey whatever is in your heart, and preferably something you imagine might be beyond their understanding. And I say this because during the lifetime of an average Japanese, it is not an exaggeration to say you could very well represent their only chance to hear a black person speak. With this in mind, my only suggestion is: please do not waste the opportunity.

Chapter 13: 25-Meter Viewing

No one is looking but everyone is watching

Please imagine walking down the street in your home-country, or anywhere outside Japan. If someone is walking toward you from the opposite direction, and it is obvious they are staring—to the point of craning their neck—would you agree this usually indicates the person who is approaching either believes they know you, or would like to get to know you? Well, in Japan, this is not necessarily the case. Many are surprised to learn that Japanese are *not allowed* to stare, look at, nor speak to strangers. The few exceptions are limited to people who are obviously lost or in need of assistance, those providing a service like passing out flyers, entertainers, and individuals who are off-code. Entertainers include singers, dancers, musicians, jugglers, even mime artists. These folks are seeking people's attention; therefore they oftentimes perform their craft in public areas where crowds are known to congregate such as parks or outside busy train stations. Have you ever been to Tokyo's Yayogi Park or Kanayama Station in Nagoya and, suddenly, caught a glimpse of an Elvis Presley impersonator? These guys sport greasy-haired pompadours with sunglasses and a white gaudy jumpsuit. Or, even worse are the middle-aged men dressed-up like members of the American rock-and-roll doo-wop group, *Sha Na Na*. As a child, I never understood this strange fascination with American idols of the 1950s but, even back then, I assumed it had something to do with some sort of post-war trauma. As for people who are off-code, they get singled-out to expose a glitch in the Japanese matrix. This type of staring is done to shame a person into adjusting their behavior; so it is a disciplinary measure. In regards to non-Japanese, considering many are devoid of common Asian features such as being short in stature with straight-black hair, it is easy to stand out in the crowd. This being said, the majority rules; so if you find yourself being eye-balled for nothing more than having astonishing good-looks, in most cases, so long as your overall actions are on-code, the person will stop staring if 'everyone' is not following suit. To do otherwise could result in the tables being turned on them for indulging in off-code behavior. So don't stare back or glare at them—that is, unless you are in an isolated, one-on-one situation. In this case, handle your business how you see fit.

Throughout the years, I have spoken to numerous young men who fancy themselves as pick-up artists. Over and over again, I have listened to stories about how they got shot-down by Japanese women after claiming they had been stared at by these same ladies from a distance. Now, I am not here to say that approaching females on the street never results in success because there are too many exceptions. I know more than a few guys who ended up dating, or even marrying, women who they met on a chance-encounter at a convenience store or a train station. However, in most of these cases, the women were either *Eigo-Hoes*, or at least individuals seeking something outside of the rigid Yamato environment. But please understand this: it is rare for a (respectable) Japanese person to engage in *Nanpa* (ナンパ), which means walking up to a complete stranger and 'hitting on them.' So why do Japanese have a tendency to visually scrutinize people from a distance but, once the person is standing nearby, then proceed to completely ignore them? This is what one disgruntled playboy wanted to know. It has already been mentioned how

Japanese must never disturb the harmony (*Wa*) of the environment; this includes refraining from talking too loudly or doing anything which may draw attention to oneself. A good example of this is the quiet, if not stoic, comportment exhibited by Japanese on public buses, trains, and subways. While it is common to see high school students wearing the same uniforms, or salary men sporting similar lapel pins known as *Kisho* (記章), address one another, generally speaking, it is considered rude to disturb anyone not in 'your group.' The constantly repeating announcements reminding passengers "to switch their cell phones to silent mode and avoid talking on it" attest to how highly not inconveniencing others is prioritized. Making eye-contact with strangers also falls into this category. While this clarifies why Japanese appear indifferent, if not cold, toward one another in public, it does not explain their proclivity to gawk at people from a distance. It has already been explained how Japanese society functions similar to the military. Back when I was a soldier, on my days off, I rarely spent any time on the post. This is because it was bothersome during my down-time to constantly have to check the rank-insignia of every person in uniform. Failure to salute an officer, even while in civilian attire, could result in being reprimanded. Therefore I had to scrutinize any oncoming soldiers from a distance—just like Japanese do. Once I ascertained the soldier walking in my direction was not an officer, only then could I relax. In my opinion, this is what Japanese are doing: they are examining people walking in their direction to decide if they are obligated to acknowledge them.

Origin of "Cool"

Although the Japanese habit of watching from a distance includes everyone, we cannot overlook the fact that, far beyond other foreigners, black people tend to get the most attention. All over the world, it is no secret the term 'cool' was created to describe the unique 'swag' of black people. Attributed to Jazz musicians like Lester Young, John Coltrane, and Miles Davis back in the 1930s and 1940s, decades later, when Be-Bop eventually evolved into Hip Hop, it is evident by icons such as *Kool D.J. Red Alert* and *L.L. Cool Jay* how the demeanor of black people remained as the common denominator of whatever makes contemporary music and fashion attractive to the young generation. All of that was said to say this: due to our remarkable characteristics, similar to a celebrity walking into a room, it is only natural for blacks to garner the most interest. Even for Japanese who are familiar with negative stereotypes regarding blacks, once in our presence, it is difficult for them not to be drawn to our melanin-rich attributes. Since the Yamato Code strongly discourages making eye contact with strangers, Japanese have learned to conceal their voyeuristic tendencies through a variety of indirect methods such as pretending to look at something near or behind the person they want to see; or another favorite, especially for females, is watching people by their reflections in the large windows of office buildings and department stores. So rest assured, just because Japanese do not appear to be looking, most likely, you're being observed at all times.

Avoid Eye Contact

Dr. Joy Degruy affirms that, for black people, greeting others (sometimes even strangers) is a normal part of the culture. This is why, following years of living in the United States, it took some time to abstain from acknowledging or observing those in my vicinity. The adage 'the eyes are the gateway to the soul' takes on real meaning here because both positive and negative energy can be transferred in nonverbal ways such as by touch or through the eyes. Back in my party-going days I can recall times when, upon entering a club, one of my friends, or myself, picked up a negative vibe and, following a brief discussion, we ended up making a hasty exit. This usually occurred within the first fifteen minutes. In a few instances, we later found out someone at those venues got shot that night. Think about it, if you ever find yourself in uncharted territory and catch enough people glaring in your direction, without a single word being uttered, this should be an alert—if you have any sense—that you might be on the 'wrong side of town.' Considering the low incidence of physical assaults or even public arguments in Japan, how then do average people, on a daily basis, unload their accumulated stress, anger, and frustration? Many seek to dump it through indirect methods like making eye contact. Since this behavior is strictly prohibited, these miscreants only target people who they believe are weaker (by society's standards) than themselves. The hardest hit groups are females, foreigners, and those who are disabled. An ideal setting for this is the morning, rush-hour commute on public buses, trains, and subways. At times, on those packed, eerily silent vehicles, the feelings of anxiety, depression, and frustration are almost palpable enough to cut with a knife. It is of paramount importance for melanin-rich residents to be consciously aware due to how we naturally attract all forms of energy. It might take a few weeks, however, I guarantee if a person makes it a habit to constantly glance around at fellow commuters, inevitably, symptoms such as fatigue, weariness, and frustration will become their constant companions. I do not want to scare anyone into thinking they must be on the alert to snub any random, old woman who pays you a compliment on your shoes. Nonetheless, all jokes aside, you should consider it. Never forget that, according to the Code, there are few acceptable reasons for a stranger to look at, or speak to you; so use this to your advantage.

Back in the 1990s, my introduction into the field of social work came through Job Corps in Edison, New Jersey. For those unfamiliar with Job Corps, it is a voluntary program administered by the United States Department of Labor that offers free-of-charge education and vocational training to young men and women ages 16 to 24, many of whom are impoverished or considered at-risk. One of my responsibilities was picking-up and dropping off Corp members so, as you can imagine, this meant I made frequent trips to project-housing areas, mostly in Central and North Jersey; but sometimes I drove into New York City, even as far as the Bronx. Most of my coworkers detested this part of the job but I liked it. Aside from the 2 – 3 hours away from the facility, these trips allowed me to see, firsthand, the environment where the kids were being raised. If I arrived with teens in the back seats, generally speaking, these trips went smoothly because the guys milling about outside saw me with their neighbors. This automatically granted me a 'visitor's pass,' so to speak. However, on those occasions when I was picking Corp members up, since I was a lone stranger they had never seen before—in addition I was wearing a policeman's uniform without the badge—I had to be prepared to encounter any of the mayhem that naturally accompanies a poverty-stricken environment saturated with desperation and despair. Broken glass, graffiti, cigarette butts, out-of-service elevators, along with the putrid smell of urine in the stairwells, not to mention the hordes of idle people hanging around, these were just some of the signs of economic deprivation.

Even for someone like me who has never lived in the projects, before stepping out of the van, nobody had to remind me to put on my 'game-face.' The moment I was spotted in my police officer-like uniform, as you can imagine, all eyes were instantly on me. These encounters were my introduction, albeit on an unconscious level, to the concepts of frequency and vibration. If I gave off the contentious vibe of a corrupt cop or, even worse, appeared to be an easy 'mark' to be taken advantage of, the visit could quickly take a downward spiral. This may be hard to believe but, in Japan, I have likewise realized the necessity of donning my exoskeleton whenever in the public eye—but for slightly different reasons. Having a background that encompasses both the military and social work, plus the experience of living in a few different countries, it is almost natural for me to contrast the mental health condition of Japan with those from a number of zip codes across the globe. While many foreigners remain fixated on the polished infrastructure: i.e. the efficient public transportation system, streets and buildings which for the most part are free of debris and graffiti, and lack of crime, I tend to notice attributes of my surroundings that some may not appreciate such as the overwhelming amount of lost, forlorn expressions among the populace, especially those who walk with their heads down; or how the elementary school children are herded together every morning to be 'marched to school' in color-coded hats and strapped to their backs are the other essential component of their uniform: the firm-sided, book bags called *randoseru*.

Of course maintaining order is the foundation of any thriving society but, similar to the Alpha vs. Beta discussion in part 1, preserving the balance is essential because anything can be taken too far. Whether in a physical, mental, or emotional form, by definition, imbalance is synonymous with illness. For this reason, I discourage blacks from taking the polite gestures and smiles of Japanese for granted and, instead, learn to search between the lines to read the unspoken story. This is only possible by understanding the Yamato Code. The importance of keeping your emotional guard intact as well as knowing how to sidestep or defend yourself from petty unpleasantries are indispensable for sustaining mental health in Japan. And, strangely enough, a key component is averting eye contact with strangers.

Chapter 14: No Macking Allowed

The tenets of Buddhism and Confucianism highlight the importance of family and communal harmony rather than otherworldly values. Although most would never argue these are positive attributes, by western standards, it could also be said they promote behavior by Japanese that is somewhat prudish or 'goody-two-shoes.' Since hitting-on or picking-up women/men is generally frowned upon, how do Japanese initially meet for the purpose of dating? With so many constraints, some people have not swayed too far from the customary *Miai* (見合い), which is the traditional matchmaking methods of using a professional *Nakōdo* (仲人) for pairing people for marriage. However, in the past fifty years, the results of questionnaire polls taken by adults have illustrated a growing trend in favor of falling in love before committing to marriage. For many wide-eyed romantics seeking true love, known as *Ren'ai (恋愛)*, although their methods for flirting appear to be updated, in reality, they have done little more than move onto another well-respected Japanese tradition: attending an arranged meeting. *Gokon* and *Konpa* are planned events at a restaurant or *izakaya* for an equal number of male and female university students or young company workers. Since *gokons* tend to be more formal, sometimes they require a venue which can seat dozens, perhaps even over a hundred participants; whereas *konpas* are usually more intimate gatherings consisting of four or five pairs of singles. Due to this method not involving the consent or opinions of parents, even if a person does not hook-up, they still can enjoy themselves engaging in conversation with eligible members of the opposite sex.

For those aspiring to date Japanese (who are members of the society), please understand it is vital to be certifiably approved by the closest associates of your love interest. This means if the person is a classmate or coworker, first and foremost, you must command the respect of the people around you. There is no way around this stipulation. Even if you end up courting someone from your karate dojo, tea ceremony class, or aerobic lesson—these are still groups; so never forget the opinion of the masses holds sway.

Faking Friendliness

At times, the protocol of not bothering others can be somewhat perplexing to those unfamiliar with Japanese culture. If you happen to strike up an interesting conversation with a Japanese person at a bar, restaurant, or even at your school or workplace, and then 15-minutes later, by chance, happen to run into the same person at the supermarket or train station, it is not uncommon for the person to brush-you-off like a total stranger. Believe it or not, this is not necessarily an indicator that he/she dislikes you. Because Japanese are required to appear reserved, if not friendly, whenever in the presence of other people, even though it may seem obvious that you and this person got along quite well, for Japanese, this is never a sure thing. There is always the chance that, in the previous encounter, *either of you* was just pretending to have a good time. To do otherwise would have disturbed the harmony (*Wa*) of the atmosphere and this is a deviation of the Code. In an interview with Nick Cannon, Dr. Joy Degruy explained how each ethnic group prioritizes a different set of values in relationships. While Japanese place the highest priority on how an individual relates to the larger group dynamic, blacks tend to prize one-to-one relationships. She talked about how in some cultures, greeting behavior may be somewhat perfunctory and how, at times, due to time constraints or other considerations it may be dispensed with altogether. However this is not the case in African culture due to the significance placed on maintaining positive regard through established personal relationships. With this in mind, it is my belief that getting the 'cold shoulder' by Japanese, which is nothing more than *tatemae* at its highest level, has a tendency to shock black people, if not hurt their feelings. That said, it is ironic how many of these same blacks have no problem employing this formality to brush aside their brothers and sisters at the mall or the train station who are trying to do nothing more than express solidarity by acknowledging them with a head-nod or a pleasant smile.

Chapter 15: "Random" Stops by Police

Whenever a black person is questioned by the police, so long as no crime was committed, at worst, this encounter should not escalate to anything beyond a bothersome, drawn-out conversation. I have never heard of any black person getting beat-up or murdered by police. Nevertheless, in metropolitan areas like Tokyo, some foreigners complain of being routinely stopped on suspicion of overstaying their visas. Once the passport has been confirmed to be up-to-date, many officers then tend to add insult to injury by insisting on a 'body-search' and inspecting the person's bag for marijuana or other such illegal contraband.

Before I understood the Yamato Code, beyond not consenting to having my bag searched, I sometimes even refused to produce any identification until they proved to my satisfaction their decision to stop me was, in fact, random. As soon as they insisted there was no bias involved, I took the officers at their word and flagged-down the nearest bystander. After all, any one of them could be a Chinese or Korean tourist. More times than not, the people I stopped would produce their identification right away amidst uncomfortable smiles and affable apologies by the officers. After two or three people's credentials were checked, only then would I show them mine. *Can you imagine a black person in the United States addressing police officers in this way?* The last time I was stopped by police was well over a decade ago. By that time, being already in the process of deciphering their code, I had learned the value of remaining patient and appearing reserved. Just implementing these simple measures allowed me to beat the cops at their own waiting game. This occurred at a bus station on my way to work.

Following my refusal to comply with their request, I just stood by quietly and waited. Since I did not become angry and attempt to argue or resist in any way, both officers seemed unsure of what to do. This stalemate lasted for over five minutes. I waited until my bus was boarding passengers before making any move whatsoever. Then I reached into my pocket. Believing I was finally retrieving my identification card, both officers looked confused when, instead, I pulled out my cell phone. After explaining how I planned to call my school so they could explain to the vice-principal why I missed my bus, without another word being spoken, I was released. To my surprise, the senior officer then ordered his partner to step in front of the bus while he knocked on the door. Once the door was opened the officer boarded to apologize to the driver and bow to the passengers for the inconvenience he was causing. Then he assured everyone aboard of my good-standing before making sure I got a seat. Since any unlawful activity is off-code, being questioned by police is never a good look. In fact it is certified grounds for being stared at by the populace. Considering just seconds ago the passengers had witnessed me being questioned, it was the officer's responsibility to provide them with an explanation to assuage any worries or concerns.

Even though the previous encounter could be viewed as a victory, when you really think about it, who has the time or patience for this nonsense on a routine basis? For any lawfully abiding person who immediately hands over their identification and submits to a search of their body and belongings, the incident will most likely be over in a few minutes. *But at what cost to the psyche?* While the victim is not subjugated to any threat of physical violence, this still qualifies as an attack on the person's character—albeit passive. Due to this type of treatment reeking of how blacks are automatically criminalized in other countries, I do not recommend allowing your body or bag to be searched. Whenever you are approached by police, first and foremost—above all else—never appear angry, agitated, or impatient. Japanese police are trained to interpret these emotions as the natural reaction of someone who is breaking the law. Here is a piece of advice that works like a charm and is surprising to most foreigners: aside from a perfunctory greeting, never, never, never even hint you can speak or understand Japanese. The more illiterate the better! On more than a few occasions, seconds after going into my slow-witted gaijin act, I have been summarily released. Even times when I was stopped in my car for speeding—*and I was speeding*—Japanese officers quickly became rattled when confronted by a fool who did not understand anything and repeatedly bowed while apologizing in terrible Japanese: "*Su-mi…sumimaasen.*"

Even if an officer speaks in English, I still play dumb by acting like I don't quite understand. I do this by asking follow-up questions which require lengthy explanations on their part. The idea is to keep the ball in their court by making them explain. You should use the most complex vocabulary, including any legal terminology you can muster: the more difficult the words, the better. Normally officers are in pairs and if one of them can speak English it is usually the subordinate. Therefore it is the officer standing in the background who is making the decisions and if he thinks— for whatever reason—the foreigner is having difficulty understanding, in his mind, the subordinate's English ability becomes suspect. For this reason, it is imperative to keep the officer talking while you remain quiet. In many instances this, alone, is enough to make both officers uncomfortable enough to let you go. Please remember that for Japanese, in any confrontation, the goal is to save-face. Thus, once an officer commits to using English, it would be almost impossible for him to recant and suddenly start speaking Japanese as this would result in losing-face. If there is any chance the officer is failing to communicate, his supervisor may become worried they are being perceived as incompetent in their duty by the Japanese bystanders witnessing the incident. And believe me, since any police-action disturbs the harmony (*Wa*), they are most certainly aware everyone is watching. Understanding this dynamic is in effect—and using it to your advantage—allows a person to stand his/her ground whenever their space is violated. And, if necessary, to even administer a little push-back.

The reason I saved the topic of police interrogations until the end of the book is because the protocol to follow summarizes how you should conduct yourself in any confrontation with Japanese. Never forget there is a 'correct way' for Japanese to behave; therefore to stand your ground and get your point across, it is imperative to follow the Code. If done correctly, no matter by whom, any Japanese person—even the police— is forced to comply accordingly or lose face, which can result in being ostracized. While cops in other countries may be 'above the law' so to speak, in Japan, no one is above the Yamato Code. Is cracking the code an easy thing to accomplish? Of course not. It begins by memorizing the script and having the ability, when necessary, to access the Japanese frequency.

Whenever you are 'randomly' stopped by police in Japan, the need to remain calm and collected has already been mentioned. Something else almost as vital is the importance of staying on offense as opposed to feeling like you have to defend yourself. From the moment any interaction with the police is initiated, each of your words and actions should match the speech patterns and gestures of not only an innocent person but, rather, a hard-working, tax-paying contributor to society. If your visa status is current and you have not committed any crime, being stopped is harassment. This having been said, in an ideal world, I would suggest that every black person who is stopped should insist on being taken to the police-box to file a complaint. However I understand most people on a daily commute cannot simply reach into their pocket and pull-out an extra ninety-minutes of time or patience to expend on such an endeavor. No matter what you decide, stay on offense by making sure you are dictating the terms. In other words, you should not be 'talked into' anything. Here is the suggested thinking process:

1. Decide where to draw the line. Are you willing to show your identification but not submit to a body-search? Or, are you vehemently against even being singled-out in public as anyone less than a law-abiding, tax paying, resident? Whatever you decide, stand your ground and do not compromise once the pressure starts building.
2. Be pragmatic in your decision for number 1. Some factors to consider are the time of day and what you are currently wearing. There is a huge difference between being stopped in the morning or afternoon while in business attire (as I was in the incident at the bus station) and being questioned at night after a few drinks. I am not saying you should automatically acquiesce only because you just left

a bar and are wearing jeans and a t-shirt. However this is something to consider.

3. Please remember that any confrontation with police will be evaluated by Japanese onlookers. This matters to the officers. With this in mind, what is the probability that during the exchange you will appear to be an innocent victim? Do you reflect any characteristics which are considered 'taboo' by Japanese? These include visible tattoos, extensive body piercings, or dyed-hair. Again, I am not suggesting just because you have a few tattoos it is a wrap and, therefore, you should meekly submit. All I am saying is you need to evaluate your situation.

4. Everything mentioned thus far needs to be sorted in your mind BEFORE you address the police. From the moment the decision to defend your human rights has been made, every word and bodily gesture must register as being on code to Japanese. The key is to remain calm and reserved. Any herky-jerky movements, agitation, or anger sullies your reputation according to Japanese standards. Take your hands out of your pockets and either fold them in front of you, or keep them by your sides (do not fold your arms). No matter how the police start the conversation, I recommend actually bowing to them and greeting them in Japanese—even if it's sloppily pronounced. Bow deeply and before coming back erect, make sure to briefly pause. It is vital that your bow, even if it is goofy, comes off as sincere and respectful. You want to appear congenial but do not smile too much. Demonstrating this level of *tatemae* illustrates to anyone who is paying attention that you respect the authority of police officers: it shows you are abiding by the Code.

5. Once the conversation begins, I recommend only speaking English. In spite of this, do not allow them to

treat you like a foreigner. Instead, you should flip-the-script by speaking to them like *they are foreigners* who can barely speak English; you should do this even if an officer is speaking fluently. The only contradiction to this rule is to insert complex vocabulary. But make it seem innocent enough—as though these are words used in normal conversation. Have you ever seen people who raise their voice a few decibels when speaking to foreigners or old people? As if by speaking louder this will somehow make them understand? For the purpose of allowing your words to reach the ears of onlookers—who ultimately are the judge and jury—you should definitely do this too. Without sounding pretentious or phony, you should orate as if you are center-stage on Broadway because, in many ways, you are.

6. If you are willing to show your identification but nothing more, of course, you can have the identification in an easy-to-reach location, such as your pocket, and quickly produce it. However this may not appease their request for a search. Therefore, upon being asked for identification, a slightly different approach is to open your bag right in front of them. As you retrieve your wallet, you want to inadvertently reveal the contents. Once they see books, files, a pencil case, a hand-towel, a thermos—the same everyday items found in the bag of any law abiding citizen—they should conclude you have a job. In Japan, having gainful employment means that you contribute to society and, therefore, are not the type of person they should be targeting. Try not to make it obvious you are letting them see inside your bag but, rather, only that you are not paranoid about hiding anything. After that glimpse inside your bag and checking

your identification, it is likely they will waive the rest of the search.

7. If they insist on performing a search, and you are against it, try not to shake your head or say 'no.' It is better to bow again and apologize. Say something like this: "*Sumimasen* but searching me is a violation of my human rights." And bow again. You can bow and apologize any number of times. The priority is to appear reserved but steadfast in your belief; therefore the more times you bow, the better. The reason this is important is because to onlookers bowing makes you appear humble, which is in direct contrast to how Japanese view those who break the law.

8. From this point if they do not ask any questions, refrain from talking and just stand there quietly. When they do ask something, in your reply, be sure to incorporate either an apology, a bow, or both. It is important to note that I have never been arrested in Japan; but whenever I stood my ground in this manner, I had already decided beforehand that I was willing to go to the station. And you should be too. After a few minutes of this stalemate, the officers normally become uneasy. At this point, you can either continue to stand quietly or offer them an ultimatum. It has been mentioned how Japan functions like the military; so if your supervisor bears a title at a school or company he/she is, in effect, the police officer's boss too. With this in mind, inform the officers how they are making you late for work and, therefore, you require a note from them to excuse your tardiness. Make sure to ask the officers to state their names for the record. Or you can do what I did at the bus station and attempt to put them on the line with your supervisor. If you happen to work at a school or a well-known company, be sure to slide that

information in as well—again, while not making it too obvious. A variation of this method is to call any (reputable) Japanese person that will vouch for you and have the police explain the incident. Even if you are having no difficulty comprehending what they are saying, this does not matter. Make them explain to a Japanese person…and check-out their reaction. Never forget that you are the one who is being inconvenienced; therefore the onus is on them to explain why you are being detained. In most cases, your supervisor or whoever is contacted will tell you to comply with the officer's request. However, unless some new information has been imparted that requires you to reconsider your position, I would suggest sticking to your guns, especially in regards to a body-search.

Some people may be thinking: if my supervisor or any Japanese person I contact is going to agree with the police officer no matter what, then why go through the trouble of even contacting them? Because 'going through the trouble' is the point; so spread that 'trouble' around by contacting others. You've already been inconvenienced, so if they are willing to allow a petty event balloon into a full-blown situation, why should you be the one who stands in opposition? If the officer really has probable cause, let him explain this to someone you are certain he respects. Furthermore, at some point, it is necessary to draw a line in the sand in regards to what you are willing to tolerate and it has to start sometime. Why not now? Once a third-party who is Japanese has entered the dialogue, everyone involved becomes duly concerned with saving-face. This usually means multiple apologies on both sides and possibly written reports even being issued. This could entail tedious communications between higher-ups who were not even present at the time and place of the incident. Never appear agitated or angry and keep apologizing and bowing…but do not shy away from turning this into an incident which requires scrutiny. When the smoke clears, you will have established the fact that being singled-out as a lawbreaker—or anything less than first-class treatment—will not be tolerated. This only means you wish to be treated just like any other law abiding citizen.

Choosing your Battles

If Japanese police are targeting people based solely on the fact they do not appear to be Japanese, no matter how you slice it, this qualifies as racial profiling: i.e. discrimination. And it should be treated as such. One of my childhood friends in the United States was a Jewish boy named, Steve. I spent a great deal of time at Steve's house with his family and I remember the level of structure and cohesiveness exhibited by the Jewish community. In addition to Jews, there are a number of ethnic and religious groups like Mormons, Amish, Muslims, and others, who reserve their right to live in harmony with—but outside of (mainstream) Christian doctrine. At that time, having bought into the rhetoric of racism being a thing of the past, I wondered why black people in America did not emulate these examples to elevate themselves onto a sovereign platform of independence. According to Steve's father it was because unlike Blacks, "Jews feel a certain responsibility toward one another. This is a characteristic that blacks have forgotten." Please keep in mind, these are the words of a Jewish father speaking to an eight-year-old black kid. To demonstrate what he meant, he went on to explain a time when a Jewish man who lived in a neighboring town was harassed by police and ended up being detained overnight. Following the man's release he filed a complaint and hundreds of Jews—even those who lived in other towns and attended different synagogues—publicly supported him. I can recall Steve's father saying: "It was the duty of every Jew in the state of New Jersey to stand up and do something." I do not recall whether or not the officer was fired or brought up on any charges but he was definitely reprimanded. From their heinous treatment at the hands of Nazis, Jews have learned that any unfair racial bias aimed at the least of their members is an assault on every one of them. Steve's father stated since blacks have endured the hells of slavery that, like Jews, they should realize that any discrimination against a black person potentially could lead to the extreme conditions of a holocaust. He claimed when any Jewish person is wrongfully stopped or questioned by police, it is mandated by their community the victim file a complaint. Even if nothing is done, the unlawful actions of the officer will be on record for everyone to see. And if, by chance, the officer is an actual bigot, his ever-expanding recorded incidents will eventually illustrate this fact. When he finally steps over the line enough times, according to Steve's father, he will then pay not only for his current transgression but also for all of the past wrongdoings. He summed it up by saying: "In the Jewish community, we are our brother's keeper."

Am I implying that blacks should be their brother's keeper?

Not really. The fact that other races and ethnic groups feel this way illustrates how thinking otherwise is not only illogical but, moreover, sheds light on the large number of blacks who are not independent or free enough to see the benefit of collective agreement. This just means they are not following a code created by them. It has gotten so bad that some blacks now believe it is only natural to be spoken-down-to or treated like a criminal—so long as the taskmaster, himself, is not black. With that being said, the idealistic side of my nature compels me to contemplate a future-scenario wherein blacks and Japanese mixed with African ancestry view themselves as a sort of extended family. Actually, this was the idea James "Source" Elmore and I had back in 1999 when we formed the Hip Hop group *AfroAsiatic*. We both lived in Hamamatsu City, which had the highest percentage of foreigners per-capita in Japan. So accordingly, in addition to James who is a brother from Chicago and myself, we had Brazilian-Japanese dancers, a Nigerian hype-man, and a Japanese-American deejay. There was also a Chinese-American guy who did not perform but was a key member of the clique. As our popularity grew in the Tokai region, our fans gradually began to reflect the cultural diversity of our musical expression. Nowadays, I am involved with the *RealTalk* platform, which is a language-communication institute created by Sterlyn Carroll. In addition to the study of international language and culture, Sterlyn manages his own food-truck a few times a week. At times, we use the truck to stage events for his students and associates, many of whom are not 'fully Japanese' and, therefore, have 'mixed' children like me. Witnessing these youth expand their linguistic and cultural horizons beyond those of their Japanese peers makes me wonder what their worldview will be like as adults living in Japan. Is it possible for melanin-rich castaways to form an alliance that is mutually beneficial for everyone involved? This does not necessarily mean having a separate group like the Mormon or Jewish communities. By forming businesses that provide services, and patronizing each other's platforms, this alone would create such a stir in Japanese society that, eventually, it could evolve into a forum that attracts the youth. This trend can be seen right now in the overwhelming Japanese fan support of Korean groups like BTS who create and perform music that is, let's face it, just copying whatever blacks are doing in the United States.

Chapter 16: Gaijin Pass

For the entirety of this book, I have distinguished the subtleties between the role of a sovereign-minded foreign-national who stands on his/her square and a commonplace gaijin. Moreover I have consistently emphasized the benefits of the former while condemning the latter. But part of mastering the Code is knowing when it's advantageous to flip-the-script and welcome the humdrum gaijin treatment. Remember the key is balance. The easiest example is anytime you need help with something. Since it is tacitly understood that foreigners are not capable of understanding the language or the Japanese way of thinking, sometimes by going right along with the stereotype and making it plain you are clueless, this will prompt someone to rescue the hapless foreigner. *And this is good.* This is especially true if you are engaged in something tedious but important such as filling-out forms/applications in Japanese, or confirming the location of an address or if you are waiting at the correct bus stop. Since assisting those in distress is an acceptable reason to talk to strangers (according to the Code), many Japanese are willing to help with the drafting of a document or understanding a displayed sign or notice. This is a courtesy paid to visitors. My mother talked about how even she was able to get a pass on her return to Japan after decades of living in the United States. Upon arriving at her stop on a busy commuter-train in Kyoto, she claims there was little response to the polite requests of a middle-aged Japanese woman asking people to allow her to pass-by as she made her way along the crowded aisle leading to the exit. Realizing at her present rate, she was not going to reach the doors before they closed, in a moment of panic, she switched to English and everyone quickly moved out of her way. According to her, anyone saying "Excuse me" (with proper pronunciation) gets much better results than by using the same phrase in Japanese.

Over the years, getting a gaijin pass has proven extremely beneficial to myself and others who are keen to the fact that if you find yourself in a sticky situation, by feigning ignorance and saying "I'm sorry, I didn't understand," in an astounding number of cases just this simple confession—true or not—has resulted in foreigners being completely let off-the-hook. In other words, playing dumb can get you out of all types of drama. In one instance, I parked in an area that was off-limits and when I returned to my car the police were in the process of having it towed. Once they ascertained I could not have possibly understood the displayed notices prohibiting parking, I added those magic words, "Sorry, I didn't understand" in purposely mispronounced Japanese. I was released with no further questions—and with no penalty. Allow me to add that, at the time of the incident, I was unable to walk without the assistance of crutches; I even spent some time in a wheelchair. However since I never filled-out the paperwork to officially register as a physically-challenged person, I was not afforded the necessary privileges that were warranted by my condition. That said, in hindsight, I should have handled the situation differently and I am very fortunate to have escaped unscathed.

Revoked Pass?

Back in 1998, I can remember exiting Jonan High School, which was located in a fairly rural area of Hamamatsu, just as two girls who attended a nearby school happened to be riding past our building on their bicycles. After catching a glimpse of a black man with cornrows their chatter came to a sudden halt as they craned their necks to gawk in my direction. Being accustomed to this type of reaction, I paid them no mind as I proceeded to unlock my bicycle. Seconds later I heard the girls scream followed by a loud crashing sound. Evidently, while the girls were staring, their handlebars had become entangled. Rushing over, I picked up the bicycles and examined their scrapes and bruises which were quite severe. As students from my school became aware of the commotion, I could see the embarrassment on the girl's faces as they refused my attempt to take them to our school's infirmary. Any black person in Japan is familiar with being stared at in this manner. In fact, this reaction is the fuel for getting a gaijin pass. But in recent years due to the steadily increasing amounts of foreign faces, not to mention having access to international platforms on the Internet such as *Instagram*, *Facebook* and *Youtube*, Japanese are not as shocked or amazed to see us anymore. Whether this development is positive or negative, I will let you decide. However, as Japanese become used to being in the presence of foreigners, please be aware the day is coming when the benefits of a gaijin-pass—such as automatically receiving 'rock star' type attention and/or status as well as the ability to play dumb—may become null and void.

Language Competency

Hypothetical Situation: A key manager suddenly dies in the Moscow branch of the company employing me. In response, my supervisor tells me to pack my bags immediately to replace him. I can expect to live in Russia—a country I know very little about—for the next two years.

Even in such a dire situation, I am sure that by the time the airplane touches-down in Moscow, I would be able to (with a foreign accent) greet people in the Russian language, as well as ask pertinent questions such as "How much does this cost?" or "Where is the nearest restroom?" However everyone does not think like this. In chapter 10, we discussed people who feel a sense of entitlement and how this even affects those who are not classified as white. Some of these gaijin have lived in Japan for decades and cannot utter a grammatically correct sentence in Japanese. Many of them, believe it or not, have little difficulty navigating the landscape of urban centers such as Tokyo or Osaka. In large part this phenomenon exists due to the high number of J-Spex, who are programmed to only communicate to Westerners in English. On the other hand, there are also immigrants who have studied the language in an academic setting and, therefore, are very proficient in not only verbal communication but also in the reading and writing aspects. And, of course, there are those who fall somewhere between these polarities. With this in mind, my advice to anyone considering migrating to another country—any country—is to at least become competent in the language at the basic 'survival level.' This should allow you to communicate and be understood. Again, much of this decision depends on your individual reason for moving here.

Self-Esteem is the Key

On numerous occasions, I have cited the work of Dr. Francis Cress Welsing. In an interview shortly before her transition, she made a statement which really caught my attention. When asked by an (white) interviewer who claimed to be against racism what she could do to assist blacks, Dr. Welsing replied the best way for whites to help is to tell blacks what white people discuss behind our backs. While I have never been fully immersed into Japanese society, being of Japanese descent has provided moments in the company of Japanese which may not be readily available for most black people. Much of *21st Century Japan Decoded* has been written with this perspective in mind. By explaining the ethics that dictate Japanese thought and behavior and providing insight into what goes on behind closed doors, it is my hope that blacks who decide to migrate here will have the best possibility of enjoying the fruits of not only this culture but, more importantly, their personal journey as a human being. This is only possible if a person has a high level of self-esteem because every worthy relationship is built on a foundation of mutual respect. For this to occur it is first necessary for a person to respect her/himself.

Karl Perera, a qualified Life-coach, teacher, as well as the author of *Self-esteem Secrets*, teaches some of the benefits of having self-esteem.

- Self-esteem can be the difference between success and failure
- Esteem can affect your thinking, causing your outlook to be positive or negative
- Esteem affects your confidence
- Your improved mindset will enable you to make better decisions
- It affects your body image and shame
- It affects your social skills vital for effective communication

- If you do not value yourself, how then will you be able to value others?
- It will affect how you take care of yourself
- Self-esteem enables you to have the right attitude to succeed at work

He also claims self-esteem affects a person's level of happiness because it can cause you to compare yourself with others. The idea of 'happiness' is purely subjective and, therefore, what floats one person's boat may sink someone else's. That said, I have never encountered a successful person who outright lacks self-esteem. Please remember 'success' is not only what the media proclaims or whether or not a person has their own page on Wikipedia. Each person must decide their own definition for success. However when we take a glance at 'real life' it is evident, for most folks, this is not the case. These days, people are heavily influenced by other people's thoughts and opinions. The easiest place to witness this is the tremendous importance placed on the number of *likes* and *views* on social media platforms. I am certain the common denominator for true and lasting success is a firm foundation of dignity and self-respect. In addition to providing insight to the nuts and bolts of Japanese society, it is my sincere hope that each and every reader now understands the vital importance of creating the space to stand on your own square, and how this is indispensable for maintaining balance in regards to mental health. And, of course, how to achieve this in accordance with the Yamato Code.

Peace, Love, and Respect!

Takuan Amaru

Final Notes

Acknowledgements

21ˢᵗ Century Japan Decoded is the culmination of nearly thirty years of analysis and observation in Japan, the United States, as well as other countries. The insights presented are renderings of lessons from numerous experiences and people from all over the globe. It is ironic that many of the people who taught me the most about mental illness are probably those who like me the least…lol! I say this because, as a young man attempting to find my place in society, more times than not, it was the naysayers—particularly from the older generation—who were trying to keep me in what they perceived to be "my place." These traumatized 'crabs in a bucket' had already been compromised, having long ago accepted their diminished roles as second-class subjects. With this in mind, I will refrain from issuing (backhanded) compliments to folks who might be offended by my doing so; but I am appreciative of the backstabbers, coons, and people of otherwise low-levels of integrity who taught me what NOT to do. *How did they do this?* By simply displaying the results of their pathetic lives: one in which the main priority is "going along to get along" with the dominant society.

Truthfully, my decision to work in the field of mental-health occurred totally by chance. I had just graduated from Rutgers University and needed a job. While in college, I befriended a young lady named Shoba Pitchumoni. Because we resided on different campuses and never had any classes together, I rarely saw her outside of the parties we frequented on the weekends. And we both loved to dance! After graduating, Shoba started working at the Children's Transitional Residence (C.T.R.), which is a facility of the University of

Acknowledgements

Behavioral Healthcare in Piscataway, New Jersey. Since she knew I already had a part-time position at the Youth Advocate Program (Y.A.P.), she suggested I apply.

The opportunity to work with preschoolers, school-aged children, and adolescents classified as "high-risk" allowed me to understand the degree to which traumatic experiences—especially during childhood—affect not only our own perceptions of ourselves but also of the world at large. A huge 'Thank You!' goes to all the children. Witnessing these youngsters, many of whom had been the victims of rape, beatings, or other types of abuse, not only heal the scars of their trauma but, furthermore, blossom into amiable, confident, and curious kids, this verified that providing a safe, nurturing environment makes all the difference in the world. In addition to Shoba and the kids, I would like to thank Dr. Steven McClendon, Dr. Jay Voss, Ms. Joyce Clark-Addison, Mr. Elijah Butler, and Ms. Charisse West-Smith (who hired me) of the University Behavioral Healthcare, along with 'Mama' Joyce, Liz, Laverne, and Mark (I still have the African Heritage Bible). And I could never pay enough homage to New Brunswick's finest: Ms. Darcella Sessomes of The Middlesex County Youth Advocate Program (Y.A.P.).

I especially would like to thank some special folks who showed me love as a child: Tomoko-san, the Brown family, Mrs. Upshur, Ms. Scott, Ms. Hughes, Mrs. Rogers, Mrs. Douglass, the Spencer family, the Srolovitz family, the Dean family, the Williams family, the Moxie family, and the Azcona family.

On the other side of the ocean:

Having taught in Japan's school system for over a decade, I am indebted to my coworkers (from pre-school to university), especially Otake-sensei, Watanabe-sensei, Morimoto-sensei, Sanjouba sensei, Murakami-sensei, Higashi-sensei, Hanatani-sensei, Yamashita-sensei (both husband & wife), along with every student I had the pleasure of interacting with in the numerous institutions of four prefectures: Shizuoka-ken, Kyoto-fu, Kagoshima-ken, and Aichi-ken.

For overall support, I cannot thank two brothers enough—especially in the technical areas. Sterlyn Carroll assisted in just about every way possible from proofreading script to editing illustrations and photos; while Eligio Maure provided the formatting of the text.

Additionally, a big shout-out goes to Niko Yoshi Kanamori (photographer), Takeshi Makabe (photographer), Ryan Francis (photographer/model) and Shane Allen (graphic designer).

The photo of the *AfroAsiatic* press conference with Mayor Kitawaki is courtesy of *Chunichi Shimbun*, Hamamatsu City Division

Recommendations

The Internet, especially via social-media, has changed the landscape for the dissemination of news and information. Unlike in the past, individuals on the ground are now able to get their message across to greater society. Movements such as *Black Lives Matter*, *Me Too*, and the *LGBTQ+* were launched and supported largely outside of mainstream media outlets. In some cases, the big-wig stations such as CNN and MSNBC were forced to provide coverage to grass-roots demonstrations or risk being viewed as outdated sources. This is good. For sports fans old enough to remember the courageous stances made by NBA players Mahmoud Abdul-Rauf and Craig Hodges, we can clearly see the improvement from the coverage given to athletic heroes of the 1990s. Back in the day, viewers had to rely exclusively on whatever the (uninformed and/or biased) commentators on ESPN decided to report. This is a far-cry from the coverage provided for Colin Kaepernick's kneel downs to protest police brutality, or the U.S. Open Tournament where Naomi Osaka wore seven different face masks (one for each round) on which she inscribed the names of Breonna Taylor, Elijah McClain, Ahmaud Arbery, Trayvon Martin, George Floyd, Philando Castile, and Tamir Rice, respectively.

For watching the news there are numerous platforms available. However, either before or after watching BBC or Fox, I highly suggest getting an alternative perspective on what the commercial platforms are—or are not—telling you. These broadcasts are available on Youtube. *Urban X (The #1 Father & Son podcast)* features Hip Hop icon, Black Dot, and his son, Malcolm. They inform viewers of trending events through a dual, melanin-rich lens which spans generations. Black Dot, who is in his fifties, provides patriarchal guidance along with old-school, street-cred as he and Malcolm bounce ideas off each other on the hottest topics. Whether or not

Malcolm's own opinions and/or the millennial way of thinking agree with, complement, or conflict with views from Black Dot's Generation X—this alone is worth the time to tune-in. For those researching our glorious past, Tariq Nasheed's documentary films, *Hidden Colors (1 – 5)*, are packed with information that does not fit the western narrative and, therefore, is largely missing from the annals of history. The topics covered, as well as the scholars in the films, are great starting-points for further investigation. If you are interested specifically in Black Empowerment, check-out the brother, Jason Black, on either of his broadcasts: *The Black Authority* or *The Business*. Both are valuable treasures of information and guidance—especially for young men. For those who have questions, concerns, or complaints, he usually opens up the phone lines. However please consider this a warning: if you elect to call into the broadcast, be in a serious state of mind and have your question or statement prepared. And whatever you do, please do not mention my name whatsoever…lol!

There are some good shows being hosted by females as well. However, since I do not regularly watch them, I don't feel comfortable throwing any names out there. But I will suggest a book by a renowned herbalist and natural-health expert, Queen Afua. *Sacred Woman: A Guide to Healing the Feminine Body, Mind, and Spirit*. Also, any of the work by Dr. Jewel Pookrum.

On the Comedy side of the game:

Corey Holcomb's *5150* and Kraig Smith's (also known as *Kraig Facts*) broadcasts provide what I really miss about the United States: just kickin' it with the homies! On my visits to

New York or New Jersey, I am always eager to accompany friends or relatives if they get a haircut because, truth be told, black barbershops may very well be the final bastion of unmitigated Black Thought. This is where political correctness takes a backseat as some of the finest minds in the 'hood' chop-it-up on whatever is trending on TV or in the streets. And just like the folks waiting for a cut, any of the cast members on these podcasts can chime-in their opinion but if they slip-up by saying something stupid—or just somehow look strange—they *will* get roasted! In between the jokes, skits, and laughter, these shows cover current events and controversial topics from, shall we say, their own unique angles.

We the People, in order to form a more perfect union, exercise our right to tell our story from our perspective. Thanks to modern technology, we are finally able to step past the 'gatekeepers and middle-men.' Being informed by us invariably leads to defining who we are in society—i.e. controlling the narrative. This ability, in my opinion, is fundamental to realizing our melanin-rich potential.

For Newcomers to Japan

Maintaining an even keel cannot be emphasized enough. And since a person's mental-health is directly affected by their physical condition, please watch what you ingest! If you are not surrounded by family it is easy to slip into unhealthy practices, almost without notice, until well after new (bad) habits have already become an issue. It is common for individuals experiencing loneliness to resort to coping mechanisms such as excessive eating or drinking alcohol. In regards to food, I stopped eating tofu and dishes containing miso a while back due to reports of unhealthy levels of estrogen. Aside from that and some commonly used ingredients with a high-sugar content like *mirin*, compared to other developed countries, Japanese cuisine is not that bad. Therefore, if you read the labels, there are a number of delicious, well-rounded options to choose from. Nevertheless, in many cases, it is what occurs between meals or after-work that starts to add up sooner than you might think. The afternoon sweets offered by coworkers and the evening gatherings at bars or *izakayas* not only stack up additional calories but, just as significantly, may assist in clogging up vital systems related to digestion and mental/spiritual wellness—particularly if a person does not drink enough water or get sufficient sleep on a regular basis.

Another word for balance is moderation. So long as a person does not overindulge, he/she should be okay. Some of the get-togethers by coworkers are more important than others. For example, *bonenkai* (end of year) and *shinnenkai* (start of year) events are somewhat traditional and, therefore, the staff of companies are expected to attend. However every *enkai* does not hold this weight so be sure to take time off to rest the vessel. For the partygoers (I used to be one back in the day), it is not necessary to go out every weekend or make an appearance at every venue. When you do go out, of course, have fun. But be sure to flush your system as much as possible with *senna* herbs or any natural intestinal cleanser. In addition to drinking lots of water, make sure to take a good multivitamin. In fact, following a night out on the town, two glasses of water and a couple vitamins—hopefully before at least a few hours of sleep—can erase the nastiest case of hangover.

Considering the effects of stress on the body, it is imperative to have an established method of exercise. This is not only for physical conditioning but also to blow off steam. Joining a gym is an option if you have the disposable income. However there are numerous free or inexpensive options such as outside parks where people run/workout. Even if it is just walking or riding a bicycle to the station, or routinely climbing staircases (as opposed to using escalators or elevators), be sure to keep the *chi* flowing. With respect to emotional well-being, in addition to a healthy diet and regular exercise, my biggest suggestion is performing a simple, daily meditation. In the words of the late NBA great, Kobe Bryant: "Just sit for 5-minutes a day, preferably in the morning, and just listen to that inner voice." For those who commute to work by train or bus, this is the perfect platform and opportunity since sitting quietly with your eyes closed abides by the Yamato Code. So please take advantage. Don't worry about whether or not you're doing it correctly. There are many books and videos available on-line and elsewhere which run-down the details. But for now, if you are a beginner, just close your eyes, inhale deeply (from the pit of the stomach) through the nose and fully exhale. Repeat. It is okay if your thoughts drift or you fall asleep. When this occurs, just reset and try again to focus inward. It's that simple. After a few weeks of daily meditation, a practitioner should notice some changes. For me, being able to ground myself and release accumulated stress caused my focus and clarity to improve by leaps and bounds. Kobe talks about having an "anchor" and how if he skipped his daily meditation, for the remainder of the day, he felt he was "constantly chasing the day" as opposed to "being set and ready for whatever may come my way." These words are analogous to the phrase "standing on your square in the eye of the storms." And it is only fitting they come from a brother who was named after a city in Japan.

Rest In Power, Kobe!

By the way, since I mentioned the discussion of the NBA's All-time G.O.A.T. earlier in the book, I'd like to put closure on that conversation. As much as I want to bestow the title onto the recently-deceased, Laker phenom, I have to go with MJ. Perhaps owing to Mike being in my generation and having watched his entire career. Nonetheless, when it comes to wholehearted admiration and respect for their deeds and achievements both on and off the court, Hakeem Olajuwon as well as Kobe Bryant are at the top of a very select list.

Conclusion

In the final analysis, Japan is not better or worse than any other developed nation. It just depends on your cup of tea. When you step off the plane it is almost impossible to not become enamored with the solid infrastructure, especially with respect to public safety and cleanliness. However this is only half of the story because adversity takes all shapes, sizes, and colors. The absence of guns, violent police officers, and pollution is revitalizing and invigorating all at once for those of us who are familiar with the trappings of an unstable environment. For this reason, it is easy to be deceived by the well-mannered etiquette, grins, and polite gestures of the populace. A few years back, I met a graduate-student who had just arrived from Ghana. I remember laughing when he referred to Japan as "the perfect place to live." Although I tried to warn him of the other side of the spectrum, he would have none of it. Well, just over a year later, I had lunch with the same young man and his wife; we were celebrating their graduation from Nagoya University. Not only had his optimism vanished into thin air, he was now angry and bitter at the very same professors, classmates, and overall environment that, in the previous year, he had proclaimed were without spot or wrinkle. Once again, I had to chuckle when he expressed how much he wanted to go home and never return to Japan because in his own words: "There's nothing special about this place!" Since his departure was in less than a month (plus he seemed to have all the answers), I dismissed the idea of responding. But as I scrutinized his tense jawline, creased forehead, and scrunched-together eyebrows and contrasted them with the smiles and sparkling air of enthusiasm I remembered him having fifteen months prior—*when he was convinced he had found heaven on earth*—I was in awe to realize how fast the novelty had worn off.

So which opinion is valid?

In this instance, both the black and the white option get trumped in favor of "a million shades of gray." The key is balance. If you walk around Japan with your nose wide-open, believing this is some sort of Utopia just because the streets are clean and the people seem friendly, you are in for a rude awakening—as this oftentimes leads to being designated as the company or school "Gaijin Mascot." On the other hand, if a person becomes so jaded, paranoid, or suspicious that everyone is out to get them, this will likely result in communal purgatory. And as we have discussed this is the worst type of Japanese punishment. Never forget the absolute law for governing is the Yamato Code and the consensus of the group holds sway. Therefore to establish a life worth living is not dependent on being overly passive to the point of allowing Japanese, whenever they see you, to play a friendly game of "pin the tail on the gaijin." Nor is it following any particular belief or political system. It is about understanding the Japanese way of doing things and aligning your attitude and actions in accordance with their code of ethics. Have the courage to set your feet and establish a square based on principle and integrity. This is the gateway to attaining peace and satisfaction within your inner sanctuary. By doing so, you can stand tall in the midst of any storm.

Peace!

References

Articles:

Bennett, L. (1995) Expectations for japanese children.
University of Missouri-Columbia. Retrieved from
http://www.socialstudies.org/sites/default/files/publications/yl
/1003/100306.html

Blacknificent Life. (2021, Sep 24). 15-year-old nigerian math
genius wins international competition. Retrieved from
https://blacknificentlife.com/15-year-old-nigerian-math-
genius-wins-international-competition/

Dillon, T. (2000, May 31). Attention: sitting next to
foreigners is forbidden. The Japan Times. Retrieved from
https://www.japantimes.co.jp/community/2000/05/31/our-
lives/attention-sitting-next-to-foreigners-is-
forbidden/#.XeIKNugzbid

Felman, A., Sampson, S. (2020, Apr 19). What is good
health? Medical News Today. Retrieved from
https://www.medicalnewstoday.com/articles/150999

Gilmour, S., Hoshino, H., & Dhungel, B. (2019, Aug 21).
Suicide mortality in foreign residents of japan. National
Library of Medicine. Retrieved from
https://pubmed.ncbi.nlm.nih.gov/31438491/

Kopp, R. (n.d.). Saving face: a little discretion can go a long way
in Japan. Asahi Weekly. Retrieved from

References

https://japanintercultural.com/free-resources/articles/saving-face-a-little-discretion-can-go-a-long-way-in-japan/

Kyodo (2019, Sep 9). Bullied japanese teen dies in apparent suicide, blames school in journal. The Japan Times. Retrieved from https://www.japantimes.co.jp/news/2019/09/09/national/social-issues/bullied-japanese-teen-dies-apparent-suicide-blames-school-journal/

McCrann, T. (n.d.) Shame, honor, and duty. Bellevue University. Retrieved from https://www.pbs.org/mosthonorableson/shame.html

Nakata, Y. (2014, Sep 25). Uchi soto and japanese group culture. GaijinPot Blog. Retrieved from https://blog.gaijinpot.com/uchi-soto-japanese-culture/

Nakata, Y. (2014, Oct 16). The honesty and facade of honne and tatemae. GaijinPot Blog. Retrieved from https://blog.gaijinpot.com/honne-tatemae/

Ndungu, T. (2020, Oct 20). Uhuru praises uon's roy alela who created smart glove for sign language. Citizen Digital. Retrieved from https://citizen.digital/news/uhuru-praises-uons-roy-alela-who-created-smart-glove-for-sign-language-348433/

Olsen, O., Kruke, B., Hovden, J. (2007, May). Societal safety: concept, borders and dilemmas. Journal of Contingencies and Crisis Management 15(2). Retrieved from https://www.researchgate.net/publication/228129832_Societal_Safety_Concept_Borders_and_Dilemmas#:~:text=Societal

%20safety%20may%20be%20de%EF%AC%81ned,of%20str
ess%20situations'%20(Norwe%2D

Roberts, N. (2015, Dec 25). Rejection and physical pain are
the same to your brain. Forbes. Retrieved from
https://www.forbes.com/sites/nicolefisher/2015/12/25/rejectio
n-and-physical-pain-are-the-same-to-your-
brain/?sh=6f37f40d4f87

Weller, C. (2016, Jan 8). Japanese people are insanely good at
standing in lines. Insider. Retrieved from
https://www.businessinsider.com/why-japanese-people-stand-
in-lines-so-well-2016-1

Young, E. (2002, Mar 15). Rejection massively reduces iq.
New Scientist. Retrieved from
https://www.newscientist.com/article/dn2051-rejection-
massively-reduces-iq/

Books:

Amaru, T. (2015) *Gaikokujin – The Story*. Nagoya:
AfroAsiatic Books

Beasley, W.G. (1995) *Japan Encounters the Barbarian*. New
Haven & London: Yale University Press

Buruma, I. (1984) *Behind the Mask*. New York: Pantheon
Books

Degruy, J. (2005) *Post Traumatic Slave Syndrome*. Portland:
Uptone Press

References

Dower, J. (1999) *Embracing Defeat: Japan in the Wake of WWII*. New York, NY: W.W. Norton & Company / The New Press

Fuller, N. (1984) *The United-Independent Compensatory Code/System/Concept Textbook: A Compensatory Counter-Racist Code*. Washington DC: NFJ Productions

Iritani, T. (1992) *Group Psychology of the Japanese in Wartime. London and New York: Kegan Paul International / The Journal of Asian Studies*

King, R. (2010) *Melanin: A Key to Freedom*. Baltimore: Afrikan World Books, Inc.

Legge, James, trans. *(1861). Confucian Analects, the Great Learning, and the Doctrine of the Mean. The Chinese Classics. I. London: Trübner*. Revised second edition (1893), Oxford: Clarendon Press, reprinted by Cosimo in 2006.

Perera, K. (2013) *Self-esteem Secrets: 12 Steps to Success*. Carlsbad, CA: Motivational Press LLC

Rice, J. (2004) *Behind the Japanese Mask*. England: How To Books Ltd.

Stead, A. (1906) *Great Japan; A Study of National Efficiency*. London: John Lane Company.

Welsing, F. (1991) *The Isis Papers: The Keys to the Colors*. Chicago: Third World Press

Williams, C. (1987) *The Destruction of Black Civilization – Great Issues of a Race from 4500 B.C. to 2000 A.D.* Chicago: Third World Press.

Movie:

Kurtz, G. (Producer), Lucas, G. (Writer/Director). (1977). Star wars [Motion picture]. United States: Lucasfilm Ltd.

Music:

Mack, C. (1994). Flava in ya ear [Recorded by Craig Mack / The Notorious B.I.G.] Flava in ya Ear [Vinyl]. New York: Bad Boy / Arista. (1994)

Wallace, C. (1994) The what [Recorded by The Notorious B.I.G. / Method Man] Ready to Die [Vinyl]. New York: Bad Boy / Arista. (1994)

PDF:

Guiding Principles for Stabilization and Reconstruction: Safe and Secure Environment (Section 6). The United States Institute of Peace (USIP). Retrieved from https://www.usip.org/sites/default/files/GP_46-70_Safe_Secure_Environment.pdf

Video:

Kobe Bryant - The Power of Sleep & Meditation. Retrieved from:

References

https://www.youtube.com/watch?v=LdrVVJPlUK4&t=203s
&ab_channel=ThriveGlobal

Additional Link:

The United States Institute of Peace (USIP):
https://www.usip.org/

Index

www.ingramcontent.com/pod-product-compliance
Lightning Source LLC
LaVergne TN
LVHW051526170726
843492LV00006B/1645